Waterways to Derby

The Derwent Navigation and the Derby Canal

Celia M Swainson

Celia M. Swainson

Scarthin Books
1993

Waterways to Derby

Preface

My interest in the use of the River Derwent for transport to and from Derby in the eighteenth century, was first aroused when researching the use of the River Trent near my home at Weston upon Trent. Letters and documents in the archives at Melbourne Hall included many with comments directly related to disputes about possible use of the River Derwent. When I decided to investigate further, the intrigues and disputes which began to emerge encouraged me to abandon temporarily the River Trent, and concentrate upon the Derwent and Derby's canal.

Although this book is the result of several years work it cannot possibly cover the whole subject; a much larger volume and considerably more research would be necessary before a definitive history could be written. However the decision of Derby City Council, through their Riverside Project, to revive use of Derby's riverside -potentially one of the city's most attractive features - prompted production of the present volume. I hope that it will not only be of interest to the citizens of Derby and visitors to the area (especially as development of Derby's riverside progresses), but also be of value to those interested in the historical development of Derby and of Midland transport systems in general. If in addition it adds to the interest in, and the enjoyment of, this presently little-used recreational resource, it will have served its purpose.

Acknowledgements

My thanks are due to the following, for their permission to use material from their archives:- Lord Ralph Kerr of Melbourne Hall; the County Archivists at the Matlock (Derbyshire) and Stafford (Staffordshire) Record Offices and all their staff who have been so helpful; the librarians of Derby City and Nottingham City Local Studies Libraries for their help.

Grateful thanks to Frank Rodgers of Holloway, Derbyshire, for permission to use his photograph of Long Bridge, Derby, John Heath for his photographs, also *Derbyshire Countryside* for permission to use their photograph of the portrait of the Rt. Hon. Thomas Coke by Michael Dahl. Photographs of features as they can be seen today are my own, as are the sketch maps - in some cases a combination of details from many old maps. Thanks to my husband for taking the photographs, also to Ken Boyce for his assistance.

I would like to record my thanks to Margery Tranter for her interest, encouragement and background information, also for reading and checking my work. Especial thanks to my husband for his support and interest without which I could not have continued.

Numbers in parentheses refer to Notes, see page 60.

Front Cover:
Junction of the Derby and Erewash Canals at Sandiacre. The Derby Canal Entrance is now blocked.

Frontispiece:
Part of the "East Prospect of Derby" published in 1728 by Samuel and Nathaniel Buck. Reproduced by kind permission of Derbyshire Library Service.
Note the five men hauling a boat towards the wharfhouse. The Holmes is still in use for recreation.

Back Cover:
Sketch map to show disposition of the various canals and rivers in the Derby area.

Contents

1 *Derbyshire and its Rivers*

Introduction

The Derwent Valley

The course of the River Derwent lies entirely within Derbyshire. Its source, on the wild moorlands of Bleaklow, is close to the county border between Derbyshire and South Yorkshire. The confluence of the Derwent with the River Trent, 'Derwent Mouth', is between Shardlow and Sawley on the border between Derbyshire and Leicestershire which here follows the River Trent, and adjacent to the border with Nottinghamshire at Long Eaton.

The summit ridge of Bleaklow forms the watershed which separates the headwaters of the Derwent from the cloughs which flow north-west to feed the River Etherow and the Lancashire and Cheshire rivers; and north-east to feed the River Don and the Yorkshire rivers. This wild area of peat moss, deep gullies and cotton grass provides water for domestic and industrial use for a large proportion of the population of northern England.

After its descent from the moors the river flows into the reservoirs of Howden, Derwent and Ladybower before continuing in a generally southerly direction within a valley bordering the eastern edge of the Derbyshire Dome, which is the central limestone area of the Peak District, often called the White Peak. The Derwent valley is mainly cut out of the shales which lie between this limestone and the Millstone Grits of the Carboniferous Period. These grits form the 'Edges' marking the eastern and western limits of the White Peak.

The river flows fairly rapidly until south of Ambergate where, as the valley widens, meanders have formed due to the reduced velocity of flow. In Derby the river changes to a generally south-easterly course and enters its flood plain, the meanders become larger, the flow generally slower and the river wider. Evidence of the formation of ox-bow lakes and levees is common - some man-made, others natural. It is here that most work has been done, with river improvement schemes, to straighten the course of the river for commercial reasons.

Derbyshire, before the advent of modern transport, always presented problems of access due to the wild nature of its topography. Steep slopes caused problems for foot travellers and pack-horses, carriages tended to keep away for the same reasons. Even horse-riders found the terrain difficult. Farey in his *General View of the Agriculture and Minerals of Derbyshire* (1811), listed 41 'Ridges or ranges of high land' and went on to give a list occupying 47 pages of 'Mountains, Hills and Eminences' in Derbyshire or on its borders, followed by 54 'narrow and Rocky Valleys, or Defiles, with precipitous Cliffs'. He also stated that '. . . full one half of the County . . . at its southern end and . . . eastern side, might rather be represented as a flat country . . .'. So it was the north of the county which presented the problems of access. These were belittled by Farey, who was a surveyor and used to travelling in difficult terrain. Daniel Defoe on the other hand, in his *Tour through the Whole Island of Great Britain* (1724-6), described the Peak as 'so inhospitable, so rugged and so wild a place', and viewed 'the black mountains of the Peak' with horror, describing the road to Matlock as 'a base, stony, mountainous road', the moors above Chatsworth as 'a waste and howling wilderness', and the High Peak area as 'the most desolate, wild, and abandoned country in all England'. He did however state that 'the vales were everywhere fruitful, well inhabited, the markets well supplied'. Another traveller who commented on the difficult terrain in north Derbyshire was Celia Fiennes, daughter of one of Cromwell's officers, and used to a more rugged life than Defoe. She journeyed on horseback through Derbyshire in 1697, to visit Chatsworth, Buxton and the other 'Seven Wonders' of the Peak. Her comments included 'its very difficult to find the Wayes here for you see only tops of hills . . . its impossible for Coach or Waggon to pass some of them . . .'. Even earlier, Charles Cotton in his addendum to the fifth edition of Izaak Walton's *Compleat Angler* in 1676, spoke of the 'large measure of foul way . . .' on the Derby to Ashbourne road and then goes on to describe, in the words of "Viator" [the Traveller], the precipitous route of the packhorse way down to the bridge in Mill Dale 'as steep as a penthouse' with 'stones . . . so slippery I cannot stand'. *(1)*

The River Derwent was the only broad stream in this part of the county which could possibly be used for access, but it was only suitable for boats to below the weir of Darley Mills just north of Derby; above this, use of boats was limited to short stretches of water. Later, the steep slopes on the valley sides made canal building an expensive proposition which would have involved staircases of locks and the accompanying water supply problems. To overcome this problem, tramways were constructed utilizing inclines to carry goods to the canals from the less accessible areas. These tramways used either horse-drawn waggons or, where the gradient was too steep, steam engines to operate inclines. The Derby canal which was completed in 1796 extended north of Derby to Little Eaton, after which a gangway with horse-drawn waggons made connections with Denby and other collieries in the area. The Cromford and High Peak railway which opened in 1830/31, designed to connect the Cromford and Peak Forest canals, was operated by stationary steam engines for the inclines, and although horses were at first used on the level they were soon replaced by locomotives. Even the builders of steam railways chose to stay within the valleys where possible, tunnelling through the hills rather than attempting an ascent. A good example of this is the line from Ambergate via Matlock, Rowsley, and Millers Dale to Buxton and Manchester, which was completed in 1863. This has many tunnels both long and short in order to follow as closely as possible the valleys of the Derwent and the Wye. As a result of the expense involved in these eighteenth and nineteenth century civil engineering projects, it was not until the advent of the motor car and reasonably surfaced roads that the more remote parts of the Peak District were fully opened to the traveller and for commerce.

Many will think this is a retrograde step, but it is an inevitable result of the process which began, in the Derby area, in the late 1600s with the desire to open up the lower River Derwent to navigation. After some years of operation the many problems encountered by boats on the river (floods, low water levels and the meandering route among others), led to proposals for a canal connecting Derby to the Trent and Mersey Canal, by this means providing speedier transport to the rest of the country. However Derby's canal was challenged within 40 years by the construction of the railway linking the town to other major centres. The railway itself has now largely been superseded by the motor car and commercial vehicles. Inevitably industrialisation has accompanied every stage of these evolving transport systems. Mills, for purposes other than simple grinding and fulling processes, were built as soon as the river was navigable into Derby. Indeed, although the first Silk Mill (1702) pre-dated river navigation, it was the easier transport of raw materials and manufactured goods into and out of the town which it was hoped would ensure Derby's prosperity.

The need for improved access into all parts of the county was precipitated by the increased demand from rapidly expanding industries for the raw materials Derbyshire could supply. The County had provided lead since before Roman times, it contained easily obtained ironstone, coal, limestone and millstones; in addition copper was mined on its western border at Ecton. Transport within and from Derbyshire was the main problem.

Derbyshire also had a plentiful supply of fast-running streams, ideal for water-wheels, which at first were used for corn mills and general grinding, but as the 18th century progressed, were used to power the ever-increasing numbers of cotton mills. By the early 1780s the Strutts and Arkwright had eight cotton spinning mills on the Derwent and its tributaries, and Francis

Hurt was expanding his ironworks beyond Alderwasley. These facts have lead to the suggestion by Brian Cooper in his book *Transformation of a Valley,* which is about the industrialisation of the Derwent valley, that Derbyshire should share with Coalbrookdale the distinction of being the birthplace and cradle of the Industrial Revolution.

It is the story of the early stages of the transport evolution which this book attempts to tell. As Charles Cotton, Celia Fiennes and Daniel Defoe tell us, the packhorse trails and carriage roads were so damaged by increased traffic that they were almost impassable and it was essential to develop another form of transport. The rivers were there, their valleys led into the heart of the county, while developing technology now facilitated construction of locks to bypass weirs and other difficult areas. It only remained to obtain Parliamentary approval of the proposals, and convince the landowners that their property would not be irreparably damaged. The canals and railways which followed river navigation in this area have been well documented, but the first stage - the rivers - has generally been ignored. It was a vital stage in transport development, and caused the most aggravation and the longest running disputes. Subsequently - perhaps as a result - canal building was not opposed so much (although the river navigators objected vigorously), railways were opposed by the canal owners (unless they were also prospective railway proprietors!), but other opposers were few. The opposition had either been worn down or had seen the prosperity which followed these developments, and wished to partake in the financial gains.

1

Early Days

Derby, situated as it is just to the south of the Derbyshire upland area and at the lowest crossing point of the River Derwent, became a strategic military and economic settlement early in its history.

The Saxon settlement of Northworthy, between the River Derwent and Markeaton Brook (which it utilized for corn mills), did not occupy the area which many years before had been the Roman camp of Derventio. This camp on the opposite or eastern side of the River Derwent was deserted about 400AD, and the earliest Saxon settlements in the Trent Valley are dated early to mid-sixth century. Danish (Viking) settlement began in earnest about 877AD and may have taken over the Saxon settlement, or developed as a new settlement which after expansion took the name of Deoraby. Both these settlements were near to the only possible crossing point of the river, the 'Causey' or 'Stoneyford'. The Romans are thought to have had a wooden bridge opposite their camp, but this had long since rotted away.

Both Saxons and Danes came up rivers such as the Trent on their initial forays and plundering expeditions, but once settlements had been established land transport was preferred and the rivers were only used very locally for trading, fishing and working mills. As Derby grew, the population (by now Christian) established religious houses and the more prosperous citizens generously endowed them with land, farms and property. In this way they sought to gain favour in after-life. Mills were built by the monasteries beside any convenient watercourse to grind corn initially, but later use was for other grinding and pressing processes. As the number of monks and lay brothers increased, the output of these mills was insufficient so weirs were built to develop a greater head of water and increase the power of the water wheels. Another use of watercourses for which a certain amount of blockage of the water flow was needed, was fishing. Weirs made of brushwood initially but later reinforced with stonework, retained the fish in a pool which made capture much easier and so provided a good food reserve. Mill-ponds of course served both purposes, and the abbeys jealously guarded their rights upon the rivers. There are reports of minor skirmishes between the retainers of the Abbot of Dale and monks from other religious Houses who wished to occupy some of the mills at Borrowash.

Prior to these problems the burgesses of Derby had (in 1204) obtained a charter from King John giving them freedom of the navigation upon the River

Derwent. It also allowed the taking of tolls on Swarkestone Bridge (the Bridge of Cordy) and from Dunebruge [Doveridge] to Estweit [unidentified - but possibly in the Erewash area]. In this case this would indicate the whole of the River Trent from the present Staffordshire boundary to the boundary with Nottinghamshire. This charter is generally regarded as confirmatory to one given by Henry II (in 1155) and was often quoted by the citizens in protection of their rights: 'navigable from ancient times . . .'. Needless to say this caused continual friction with Dale Abbey regarding use of the River Derwent; but the Abbot seems to have retained his mills at Borrowash, in fact in about 1268 he is reported to have had nine mills in the Borrowash area! *(2)*

At the Dissolution of the Monasteries the lands, mills and weirs belonging to the abbeys merely passed into other hands. Robert Sacheverell, a son of the Sacheverells of Morley, acquired Darley Abbey; and some of the Borrowash and Spondon properties of Dale Abbey were purchased by an ancestor of the Wilmots of Chaddesden and Osmaston. The mills continued to operate with the weirs still obstructing navigation of the river.

The other obstruction to clear passage of the River Derwent was at Wilne. Here the revenues of the manors of Sawley and Wilne which were attached to the Prebend (or benefice) of Sawley, were part of the living of one of the members of the Chapter of Lichfield Cathedral. The Domesday Book mentions Sawley Mill, which is presumed to be on the site of the present Wilne Mills. After the Dissolution these manors and the mills were acquired by the Stanhopes of Shelford, later of Elvaston, ancestors of the Earls of Chesterfield and Harrington. At one time there were reported to be six mills at Wilne - four cloth or fulling mills and two 'grist' or grain mills - with the inevitable weir. *(3)*

That was the situation which prevailed during the early 1600s when Derby's mayor and burgesses first began their campaign to open up the river to navigation from the River Trent to Derby.

It is interesting to digress here and explain the involvement of some of the characters and families, for at times the campaign degenerated into personal battles, both legal and physical.

In addition to the Sacheverells and Wilmots other families who bought monastic lands along the lower Derwent, thus becoming riparian landowners, included the Stanhopes and Allestrys. It was the Wilmots and Stanhopes who were the most active in opposition to river use for navigation.

The Wilmots of Osmaston were descended from the family who owned Chaddesden Hall. They were related by marriage to the Gresleys of Drakelow, Harpurs of Calke, Cokes of Trusley, Sacheverells of Morley and the Bembridges of Lockington. The most important members of the family involved in the navigation issue, were the Robert Wilmots. Robert (we will call him 'senior') lived from 1640 to 1722. He was High Sheriff of Derbyshire in 1689 and a Member of Parliament for Derby from 1690 to 1695. He was the elder son of Sir Nicholas Wilmot, the first Wilmot of Osmaston, and Dorothy a daughter of Sir John Harpur of Calke. Robert married Elizabeth Eardley of Eardley Hall in Staffordshire and had a large family. His eldest son, another

Robert (called 'junior' in our story) was the main organiser of opposition to the opening of the River Derwent to navigation. To assist this opposition he called upon his extensive family connections by marriage, and his father's acquaintances from Parliamentary days. These made it easier for him to lobby at the Court of George I. [Problems can often arise when trying to trace these families due to the practice of always naming the eldest son after his father, so we find a line of at least six Robert Wilmots from 1640 to 1808]. The Wilmots of Osmaston owned lands in Shardlow and the lower Derwent valley as well as other estates. They were also closely related to the Holdens of Aston, Shardlow and Wilne. *(4)*

A close friend of Robert Wilmot senior, from his days as a Member of Parliament, was Philip Stanhope who was also a Member before succeeding to the Earldom of Chesterfield. Philip, the third Earl of Chesterfield, was a descendent of Philip, one of the sons of the Sir John Stanhope of Shelford and Elvaston already mentioned. John Stanhope had divided his estates between his two sons, Philip who inherited Shelford and Bretby together with the Sawley and Draycott estates, and John who inherited Elvaston. This Philip became the first Earl of Chesterfield and John's descendants became the Earls of Harrington. Philip, the third Earl of Chesterfield, was the father of Philip Dormer Stanhope, a politician, wit and prolific letter writer. His letters to his illegitimate son have become famous as the 'Chesterfield Letters'. This literary gift was also possessed by his father whose letters to Robert Wilmot junior are a delight to read.

2 *Elvaston Castle, home of the Stanhope family. Now part of the Elvaston Castle Country Park.*

Two people who were also closely involved in the controversy (and who incidentally changed sides), were Thomas Coke of Melbourne Hall and Leonard Fosbrooke of Wilden Ferry and Shardlow. Thomas Coke was descended from the Cokes of Trusley. His great grandfather was Sir John Coke (younger son of the Trusley family) who was Principal Secretary of State to Charles I before the Civil War, and leased a house at Melbourne from the Bishops of Carlisle. The house was purchased later and in 1633 the Cokes of Melbourne bought the manor of Castle Donington. Both Sir John Coke and his son, Sir John, died during the Commonwealth. Sir John the younger was in exile in Paris, so never lived in the house, and his brother Thomas inherited it. Thomas's son (Colonel John Coke) was active in the Revolution of 1688, which brought William and Mary to the throne, and when he died his son Thomas inherited. This Thomas Coke (1674-1727) was a Member of Parliament for Derbyshire until being made Vice-Chamberlain to both Queen Anne and George I (from 1711 until his death in 1727). Since he owned the manor of Castle Donington he was also the owner of Wilden Ferry, which was a vital river crossing on the road from Derby to Loughborough and thence to London. This ferry was based on the southern bank of the River Trent at the site of the present village of Cavendish, and so controlled all River Trent traffic.

3 *Melbourne Hall, home of Thomas Coke.*

The Fosbrookes were descended from a family of mercers and river traders based at Trent Bridge, Nottingham, who in 1609 signed an agreement to carry coals down the River Trent to Gainsborough for Sir Percival Willoughby of Wollaton. Some of the family moved to Bothe Hall, Sawley, and became involved in the lead industry at Wirksworth in addition to being carriers on the River Trent. It was a Leonard Fosbrooke from this branch of the family who bought the house called 'The Homestead' overlooking Wilden Ferry and the Back Lane to Castle Donington in 1641. This house is reputed to have supplied post-horses and to have had overnight accommodation. The Fosbrookes leased Wilden Ferry from the Cokes from about this time until 1743. This Leonard Fosbrooke is the first in a line of at least six Leonards who gradually rose in society. The first Leonard died in 1670 and his son, Leonard, bought land in Shardlow between 1680 and 1684. Shardlow Hall was built on this land (see pictures, page 16), its grounds stretching down to the River Trent opposite the Homestead. This second Leonard (we will call him 'senior') was quite an old man when the final skirmishes for the River Derwent navigation took place. His writing is very shaky and difficult to read but he was intensely loyal to his son. He sent repeated letters to Thomas Coke pleading his son's innocence when trouble developed at the ferry. The third Leonard ('junior') was the person most involved in their side of the Derwent

4 *Probable site of Wilden Ferry, showing the village of Cavendish and the remains of the first Cavendish Bridge.*

5 *(right) Shardlow Hall, the present south-east frontage as seen from the A6 road.*

6 *(below) Shardlow Hall, north-west frontage, possibly as built by Leonard Fosbrooke.*

navigation dispute. He seems to have been active in the working of the ferry and wharf areas at first, but as his father grew older he appears to have been less involved in the manual work. He was always *very* innocent when any trouble arose. His explanations of incidents are most amusing to read, for example: 'we saw their Mallice so hott . . . I never spoke words to any of them . . . I can positively prove a Riott & an assallt upon me . . . but they are inventing what mischeife they can against you as well as us . . . I finde theire couridge will quickly faile if once opposd . . .'

Gradually he withdrew from the ferry work; the last time it was leased to him was in 1722, for 21 years at £68.10 shillings per annum. After this (1743) the ferry was let to the 'Derby Navigators' - a consortium headed by Sir Thomas Gisbourne and Samuel Crompton (of Crompton and Evans Bank). This withdrawal from involvement with the ferry may be linked with the fact that in 1725 Leonard Fosbrooke junior, was High Sheriff of Derbyshire, quite a rise in status. In about 1800 the Fosbrookes sold Shardlow Hall to James Sutton who was involved in the Trent and Mersey, and Derby Canals. The Fosbrooke family had bought the manor of Ravenstone in 1741, where they pulled down the old Manor House and built a smaller one, and then moved there to live. The Soresbys, originally river carriers, and Suttons were the families most involved with the canals around the Shardlow area.

It was on 12th January 1633 that King Charles I granted a 'Lease of the passage by the water . . .' on the River Derwent to Thomas Statham on behalf of the Gentlemen, 'Bayliffes and Burgesses of the said towne of Derbie . . .' for thirty-one years. The rental was £10 yearly with the condition that the river was made navigable 'from ye Trent to Derby and thence to Crumford . . .' with all possible speed. The parchment was signed by Sir John Coke, as Secretary of State. The project was obviously more difficult than had been envisaged because letters to Sir John Coke in 1637 indicate work had not begun. On 6th April 1639 the King recommended (through Sir John Coke) that the Corporation of Derby offer accommodation to Sir Cornelius Vermuyden and accept his advice on the project. Vermuyden, the Dutch engineer, had already worked on drainage of the Fens of Lincolnshire and South Yorkshire and also on drainage of the Derbyshire lead mines, and the King obviously thought he would be able to advise the Derby burgesses. National events however, overtook them, the Civil War broke out in 1642, and the project was shelved. *(5)*

During the period of the Commonwealth there were very few attempts to obtain Parliamentary backing for any river navigation projects; only two River Navigation Acts were passed for the whole country and the River Derwent was not one of them.

2

After the Commonwealth

After the lull in Parliamentary river navigation activity during the Commonwealth, it was only natural that when King Charles II came to the throne the pro-navigation lobby were overjoyed and became very active. However there seem to have been phases of almost frenzied activity when river navigation was fashionable and many Acts were passed, followed by times when Bills were vigorously opposed.

On Saturday 10th November 1664 a Bill for Navigation of the River Derwent was presented to Parliament, it was read for the second time the following Tuesday (13th November) and was to be studied in Committee of the House of Commons after Christmas. The Bill never became Law even though this was one of the 'fashionable' periods.

Opposition to use of rivers for transport increased in the late 1660s and 1670s, and a further attempt to get a Bill through Parliament in 1675 failed, again at the Committee stage. The House of Commons Journals which report this on the 6th and 7th November 1675 have an interesting entry for the previous day (5th November) when Parliament 'ajourned' and went to St. Margaret's Church, Westminster, to hear a sermon on the Deliverance from the Gunpowder Plot! It was at this time that Nottingham Borough Council started to organise opposition to any river transport above 'Nottingham Bridges'. This opposition was at first against an extension of navigation upon the River Trent, but was extended to oppose any other navigations which were proposed (eg. Derwent, Soar). It was to increase in intensity and continue until finally the Act for Navigation on the River Derwent was obtained. It re-emerged in the 1880s when the whole River Trent navigation was taken over by the Nottingham Corporation. This opposition was due to Nottingham's determination to remain the dominant town in the area and the 'head' of navigation on the River Trent. *(6)*

A gap of 20 years now appears before the next attempt, but it is not clear whether this was due to lack of finance or enthusiasm. However the Nottingham Borough Council must have had prior notice of the next application because they arranged an informal meeting on Tuesday 17th December 1695 at 'Mistriss Johnson's' - possibly a coffee house - to draw up a petition to be presented to Parliament. The day after this meeting John Bagnold, one of the two Members of Parliament for Derby, presented a Bill to Parliament for the Navigation of the River Derwent. Again it was read a second time and passed to the Committee which was inundated with petitions both for, and against the Bill. Nottingham got theirs in first, on the 7th January. They claimed that the grounds for the Bill 'were fallacious' - the Bill claimed navigation on the Derwent would improve trade generally and increase the supply of seamen for the Navy (England and much of Europe were at war with France at this time and the English naval victory off La Hogue in 1692 was still very much in people's minds). Nottingham's petition stated that river navigation would not produce one seaman in 20 years! These arguments were frequently used for, and against, river navigation in general not just in the Midlands. The burgesses of Nottingham also maintained that to make the rivers navigable above the Nottingham Bridges would ruin the trade of the land carriers. Other opposers included the Mayor and Burgesses of Leicester, the town of Bawtry (who feared damage to their trade in lead and millstones from Derbyshire), the inhabitants of Radford, Bramcote, Sandiacre, Stapleford, Long Eaton, Attenborough, Worksop, Northampton,

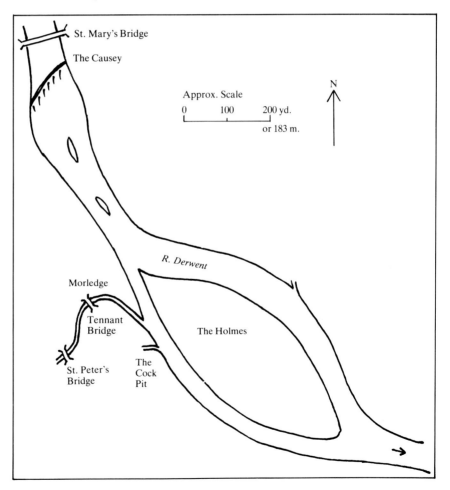

7 *Derby and the River Derwent before 1720.*

Sr   Janry: 24 wtb99

mr Bagshaw brings & wth him to London Copyes of
the three Bills of Inditemt: against my Son & the rest
I wish you would please to Reade them, may there in
observe there Indeavours to have pt: of the River in
Darby Shire, besides the verditt against mr Houlden
there found a writeing of great Antiquity wth I shew
to Serjeant Bigland yesterday & hee may be of great
use to you & Occasion, mr Bagshaw hath a Copy of
one of Sr Henry Cary & mr Corbett warrants, if you
please to Reade that, the other was found out of still a Co
of, that was as I was told to take any that should oppose
the Darby men in Landing Goods, mr Bagshaw hath a
Past of Attor. & severall dayes proceedings & if Bag
shaw & the Cunstable of Donington takeing a distress
& others to Reing, if it from him, wth their hands
to attest it, procured the Opinion of Sr Bartleme
Shore to Concurr wth Serjeant Biglands to proceede aga
them, wth mr Bagshaw hath a Copy of, if you please t
Reade them, I am told from a good hand the Darby me
have soe farr gott the favour of yor: Tennents & my
Neighbours at Donington that the are for discharging
most of the boate houses & ferry yard, leaveing you only
a boat for the ferry man, & this is said to bee, because
you are unkind in these times, Good mr Coke Keep this
to yor: Selfe Lest I become the Client of there hatred
wth indeed I am to all yor: adversaries for espousing
yor: right wth not wthstanding I will not depart
from, if you please to Incourage mr Bagshaw there
is noe feare of putting a Stop to them this terme,
wth I hop you will doe, that my Selfe & Son may doe
bee easy, I should bee extreamly glad to heare from
you, that am & shall bee remaine

yor: faithfull Humble
Servt; Jo: Holbrooke

Loughborough, Scarsdale, Chesterfield, East Retford, Blythe and also 14 of the Grand Jury of the Quarter Sessions of Peace in Derby. Petitions in favour of the Derwent Navigation Bill came from the High Sheriff and the remaining Justices of the Peace of the Quarter Sessions in Derby (ie. they were divided, so sent one petition for and one against!), Lichfield, Burton upon Trent, Kegworth, Shepshed, parts of Loughborough, Birmingham, the leadminers and merchants (transport would be easier than via Bawtry), Newcastle under Lyme, Uttoxeter, Middlewich, Nantwich, and also from the Lead Merchants and Cheesemongers of London and Westminster (who considered their transport costs would be reduced considerably). It is noticeable that the opposers are mainly from a limited area whereas the petitions in favour of the Bill come from a much wider area of the country. The final petition on 14th February 1696 was from several Burgesses and Inhabitants of Derby who claimed the Bill was brought in due to the influence of 'a few Maultsters and petty chapmen of Derby who mind more their own private gain than the general good of that town ...' and plead 'that the Town of Derby be not its own Ruin ...'. This seems to have been successful because the Bill was rejected. *(7)*

It was during this time that the tradesmen and some of the inhabitants of Nottingham offered to pay one third of the costs incurred by the Borough in fighting the Bill. The Corporation of Nottingham thankfully accepted but asked for half the costs, the Corporation would then pay the other half. This shows a general concern amongst the inhabitants of Nottingham who had realised the importance which accrued to their town by reason of its position at the head of a navigable river. The whole town seems to have been united in its opposition to any extension of navigation - or loss of prestige.

During the whole of this time, Nottingham was also fighting proposals to extend navigation of the River Trent as far as Burton upon Trent, so more drastic action was necessary. On 30th August 1698 the Borough Council decided that all boats from Sawley and Wilne should be stopped at 'Trent Bridges' and in order to ensure this, the arches of the bridge should be 'chayned and stopped vp [up]'. It was also ordered that two men should assist the town's constable in noting the names of owners of boats and also of those 'who hayle the same ... for their trespassinge upon the Towne's ground' (at this time boats were hauled by teams of men - as the use of horses was not allowed until 1783). A law suit followed, but since boats continued to use the Trent as far as Wilden Ferry, Nottingham must have been unsuccessful.

On 20th November 1698 the Mayor and Burgesses of the Borough of Derby sent a petition to Thomas Coke, who was a Member of Parliament for the County, stating their intention to 'obtaine an Act of Parliamt. for makeing the said River [Derwent] Navigable ...'. They requested his assistance hoping that he would 'preferr a publik good before any private Intrest of your owne ...'. Word of this petition must have reached Nottingham because two days later the Corporation was resolving to oppose it, and proposing to write to various surrounding villages and towns (including Boston, Lincoln and Hull) to request their support. *(8)*

8 *(facing page) Letter from Leonard Fosbrooke (senior) to Thomas Coke, 1699. Reproduced by kind permission of Lord Ralph Kerr.*

In December of that year Leonard Fosbrooke (senior) wrote to Thomas Coke, reporting that the Members of Parliament for Derby (George Vernon and Lord Henry Cavendish) were in favour of the Derwent Navigation. However at this time he was more concerned with the imminent Bill to make the River Trent navigable as far as Burton upon Trent (passed 1699) and the protection of his rights on that river. Thomas Coke was contacted by a number of local landowners, all concerned about (and opposed to) the proposed Derwent Navigation. Walter Burdett of Foremark when he sent a petition to solicitors in London said, 'I do not heare of one Gentleman yt [that] is for making Darwent Navigable but I hear ye projectors use very foule practice of wch I'll tell you more when I see you'! Sir Gilbert Clarke of Chilcote (Leicestershire) wrote to Thomas Coke 'I thinke it is very proper for those whose interest it is to bee against the makeing Derwent navigable to joyne in a petition as you direct ... but for my owne part, haveing no land upon that water and haveing so much disobliged the town of Derby allready I am not willing to signe any paper'. The records do not say what he meant by this! *(9)*

Leonard Fosbrooke could see that the Burgesses of Derby were determined to get their navigation so he suggested to Thomas Coke that since they already controlled the River Trent by their river ferry crossing at Wilden, they should also build wharves and warehouses at a convenient spot so that they would have some control of the trade on the River Derwent.

The great concern expressed at this time was that the river carriers would be able to control prices at Derby markets, especially the price of corn which fluctuated frequently. Although there was general agreement that the landowners would be compensated sufficiently for any damage to their land - the Derwent was not the first river in the land to be proposed for navigation - nevertheless the landowners still remained apprehensive. Petitions in favour of the Navigation Bill came from the Ironmongers and Cheesemongers of London who spoke of the problems they had at Wilden Ferry, but the landowners petitioned against. Between the first and second readings of the 1698/99 Bill, Leonard Fosbrooke sent lists of petitioners with details of their land (if any) on the Derwent, their occupation and some personal details. 'Mr. Tho Allestry ... hee hath pretty deale of land on Derwent, Wm. Robbinson hath about £30 pr. annum, but little on the Derwent, Richard Moore, wee knowe noe such person, Richard Stenson is a Showmaker [shoemaker] & onely keeps 4 or 5 cowes, John Jordon a very poore man, James Holland holds nothing only ye house he lives in ... Most of the rest are alehouse keepers, day laborers or small farmers'. This list which shows few petitioners were landowners, must have helped to swing opinion in Parliament against the Bill which was rejected in 1699 before getting to the Committee stage. *(10)*

3

Wilden Ferry and the Cheese Trade

Meanwhile Leonard Fosbrooke was having trouble at Wilden Ferry. Certain prospective river carriers had obtained wharfage from Lord Chesterfield at Sawley (down-river from Wilden) and were trying to take over the cheese trade which Fosbrooke regarded as his own. Cheeses collected from a large area of Derbyshire, Staffordshire and Leicestershire, were brought to Shardlow by road for carriage down the River Trent to Gainsborough and thence round the coast to London. This was a very lucrative trade, so the 'Sawley Navigators' (sometimes called the 'Derby Navigators') tried to get up-river above Wilden Ferry to the cheese wharf and load their boats. Fosbrooke, junior, wrote complaining bitterly to Thomas Coke but before he could get a reply the Derby men acted, bringing a Magistrate, 'Jaylor' and the Derby Constable with them. They 'came into our Cogg Boates' and pulled Fosbrooke's men out on to the Derbyshire bank where they were served with warrants and bound over to appear at the Sessions the next day (see page 20). Fosbrooke's men were accused of causing a 'Riot' the first time the Derby men tried to pass the ferry, but according to Fosbrooke his men were on the ferry not on the Derbyshire bank at the time. He himself was in the ferry yard 'about my busyness . . .' and did not speak to the men. However he was accused of assaulting a certain William Parker, but he only 'gave him a thrust wt [with] my elboe to prevent him going along ye Plank wth Cheese from ye shoare and in this ye evidence accknoledgd yt [that] Parker gave ye first assallt upon me . . .'. For this reason Fosbrooke accused the Derby men of 'a Riott and an assallt upon me'. He summoned the Castle Donington Constable but failed to catch the men on the south (Castle Donington) bank of the river. He reported to Thomas Coke a rumour that the Derby men had written to Lord Huntingdon (owner of Donington Hall) for his help to obtain permission to carry on business from the south bank of the River Trent, making similar promises about the profits to be obtained as they had done when petitioning Lord Chesterfield for wharves at Sawley. Problems with the Derby men continued for almost a year with accusation and counter-accusation. Leonard Fosbrooke, junior, thought he could control river traffic by refusing to lower the ferry rope, which was necessary in order for boats to pass. He reported to Thomas Coke that the Derby men produced a 'hatchett . . . but durct [dare] not make use of it . . .'. His father wrote to Thomas Coke 'as I remember there was in some Tryall as I have tould evidence given that noe Boates but those belonging to Wilden ferry was permitted to goe about the Rope ...'. They also found that the Derby men were attempting (unsuccessfully) to get a lease for a wharf on the Trent from Lord Pagett, who had been made the Undertaker of the Trent River Navigation in the Act passed at the end of 1699. *(11)*

The court cases which resulted from this activity alerted various people to

9 *Letter from Leonard Fosbrooke (junior) to Thomas Coke, 1699. Reproduced by kind permission of Lord Ralph Kerr.*

the fact that Thomas Coke and the Fosbrookes might not have any legal right to exclude other river carriers from the Shardlow area. Solicitors began to question Thomas Coke's title to the river navigation and decided that he only owned the ferry at Wilden and fishing rights. However in order to prevent a law suit in London and the possible scandal, it was suggested that lease of the ferry should be shared between the Fosbrookes and the 'Derby Men'. The negotiations resulted (in 1701) in a shared lease between Leonard Fosbrooke and the Mayor and Burgesses of Derby, soon followed by an agreement between Thomas Coke (together with Fosbrooke) and William Parker of Derby, gent. (together with Thomas Bingham of Derby, mercer). If this is the same William Parker who Leonard Fosbrooke thrust with his 'elboe' only a year before, it is surprising how quickly these young men become 'gent' - respected members of the community! The cost of the shared lease to both parties was £31 twice yearly for which it was agreed they were all permitted to carry goods on the River Trent from Wilden to Gainsborough. Leonard Fosbrooke was to keep the money from the ferry but Parker and Bingham were to have rooms in dwelling houses near the ferry as well as wharves and warehouses on the south bank of the river. Non-payment within 40 days of the Feast of St. Michael the Archangel and the Feast of the 'Annunciacōn' of the Blessed Virgin Mary, would lead to forfeiture of the lease. *(12)*

Meanwhile Thomas Coke had received a letter which although it is readable, has been mutilated - the name of the sender and the final signature have been removed. This contained veiled threats to Thomas Coke's re-election to Parliament in the coming elections and suggested that unless he supported the writers in their efforts to obtain a Derwent Navigation Bill, Lord Rutland would be proposed as the County Parliamentary Representative. However both Thomas Coke and Leonard Fosbrooke considered that the River Derwent would never become navigable and were still in opposition to any further attempts. *(13)*

In the spring of 1702 Fosbrooke, junior, wrote to Thomas Coke to inform him that Derby Corporation was once more preparing a Bill, 'Mr. Sarracoald putting them upon it who goes up for London as I am informd this day & presume may come to you about it as soone as he comes . . . last night when I came away from ye Asizes Mr. Sarracoald was to treat ye Hall at his owne house . . .'. This was George Sorocold (the famous engineer) who is noted for the London Bridge works, the first Liverpool docks, the first wet dock at Rotherhithe, Derby Silk Mill and the first piped water supply at Derby as well as plans for the River Derwent Navigation (see page 26). Fosbrooke must have been very upset not to be able to report to Thomas Coke on conversations between Sorocold and the Derby Corporation at Sorocold's house that evening! (the 'Hall' was the meeting of the Mayor & Burgesses - the 'Town Council'). He was also upset at the idea of another application because Thomas Coke had promised to build him a new ferry boat. Fosbrooke could not see the value of a new boat if the Derwent became navigable because traffic on the roads and ferry would decrease, so reducing his income. *(14)*

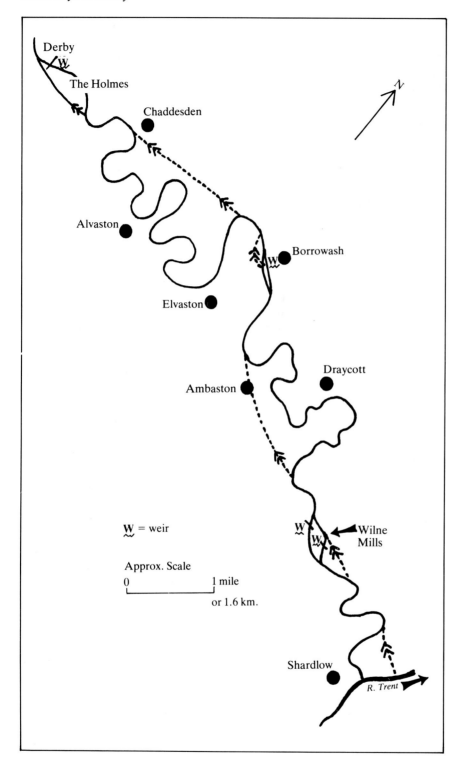

10 *Possibly the way George Sorocold proposed to straighten the River Derwent in 1702.*

Derby

W

The Holmes

Chaddesden

N

Alvaston

Borrowash

W

Elvaston

Draycott

Ambaston

W = weir

Approx. Scale

0 ———————— 1 mile

or 1.6 km.

W

Wilne
Mills

W

Shardlow

R. Trent

The two Members of Parliament for Derby, John Harpur and Thomas Stanhope, prepared a Derwent Navigation Bill which was supported by a petition from the Mayor and Burgesses of Derby, in November 1702. Nottingham Corporation again swung into action requesting that their Members of Parliament oppose it and petitioning Sir Thomas Willoughby of Wollaton Hall for his assistance. They also contacted the Earl of Chesterfield. The Corporation voted to allow £40 'towards making a vigourous Opposition agst the sd Bill . . .'; it was also 'Ordered that Mr. Mayor and the severall Aldermen do take as many as they think fitt along wth them and go through their respective Wards and collect what money they can towards opposing the River Darwent'. They sent a petition to the House of Lords when the Bill passed the Commons and sent some Aldermen 'to prove this Corporacions Peticon before the Lords'. George Sorocold also went to the House of Lords to speak in favour of the Bill and to produce his proposals. He suggested short cuts and locks to avoid the weirs and two long cuts to bypass the large meanders which are a feature of the lower River Derwent. The Lords rejected the Bill on 1st February 1703 to the great relief of many, but the chagrin of the citizens of Derby and their supporters. *(15)*

Meanwhile Thomas Coke and Leonard Fosbrooke had built the new ferry boat for a total cost of £142.2.6d. They agreed to share the cost of the boat but Fosbrooke paid for new stanchion posts. They had also come to the conclusion that Derby would eventually get their Bill, so they began to prepare for the inevitable. They would no longer oppose the Bill, but they would not let the other opposers know of their change of heart. This caused a few problems when the final Bill was passing through Parliament. *(16)*

In 1709 Derby Corporation were late with paying their share of the lease on Wilden Ferry and Leonard Fosbrooke took over the whole lease on 2nd February 1710. He also repossessed the houses and land he had been required to allow the Derby Corporation representatives to occupy. Subsequently, in June 1710, he entered into a most lucrative agreement with the Cheesemongers of the City of London which gave Fosbrooke the sole right to carry cheeses from a large area of surrounding country to Gainsborough for shipment by sea to London. The cheeses were to be brought to Wilden Ferry 'in the County of Leicester' (ie. not the Shardlow bank of the River Trent, where river carriers from Derby might attempt to 'pirate' his trade) and would be carried down river 'with as quick desptch as the Weather will permitt . . . Inevitable accidents as ffloods to prevent the same only fforeprized and excepted'. If any cheese was not transported within ten days, transport would be free. All the Cheesemongers promised that Fosbrooke would be the sole carrier, only cheeses already agreed to be sent to 'Nottingham Bridges' were to be excepted. The payment was to be 12 shillings for every 'Two and Twenty Hundred weight' until 10th May 1711 and in proportion for greater or lesser quantities after which it was to be 11 shillings for 7 years. A certain 'Samuell Waters' was appointed as agent at Wilden Ferry wharf to check in the cheeses and pay for their carriage, for which he was to be paid 2 shillings per 'Tun . . . accompting [accounting] Two and Twenty Hundred to the Tun'. Then he was

to notify the London Cheesemongers of the despatch of their cheeses. This 'Tun' is an interesting measure, assumed to be a very local one and possibly relating only to the cheese trade. The large document of this agreement is signed by 58 Cheesemongers all with their individual seals and countersigned by William Fox (Steward of the Manor of Castle Donington for Thomas Coke) and Samuel Waters (the agent) as witnesses. Thus, although the Cheesemongers had no doubt obtained preferential terms for transport of cheeses, Leonard Fosbrooke had a guaranteed steady income and it is this sort of business agreement which helped him and his family to rise up the social ladder so that by 1725 he was High Sheriff for the County. *(17)*

In January 1705 Leonard Fosbrooke, junior, bitterly accused Thomas Coke of letting him down by not notifying him of an imminent River Derwent Navigation Bill. This one letter however, is the only evidence of a Bill and it was probably a false alarm. No further attempts were made to obtain Parliamentary backing for navigation on the River Derwent until 1717, by which time the citizens of Derby were beginning to feel the tide was turning in their direction.

Thomas Coke became Vice Chamberlain to Queen Anne in 1711, a position he also held during the reign of George I. This meant he ceased to be a Member of Parliament for Derbyshire, so he need not take notice of the wishes of the electorate especially the River Derwent Navigation lobby. Similarly, Thomas Parker (later Sir Thomas Parker) who was one of the Members of Parliament for Derby from 1705-1710 was made Lord Chief Justice of England in 1710 (so that, like Thomas Coke, he no longer needed re-election). He assisted the introduction of this 1717 Bill. In 1714 there had been an election which produced a violent contest in Derby. The sitting Members for Derby, Edward Mundy and Nathaniel Curzon, both opposed making the River Derwent navigable, this inevitably meant they were not re-elected. They were replaced as the Derby Members by the Hon. Lord James Cavendish and Sir William Stanhope, both of whom were in favour of navigation on the River Derwent. The Bill which was introduced by these Members in 1717 was claimed to have the support of most of the riparian land owners such as Lord Ferrers, Lord Chesterfield, the Lord Bishop of Lichfield and Coventry, Lord Newport and Sir Robert Corbett. (It should be noted that Lord Ferrers and Lord Chesterfield both opposed the next Bill in 1719 claiming they had been mis-informed). Nottingham Corporation again petitioned Parliament against the Bill. This time they voted to contribute £100 towards the opposition 'by reason itt is apprehended if itt should passe the same will be of very Ill Consequence to this Town and Corporacon'. Once again the Bill was rejected but the opposition was decreasing, more rivers having been successfully made navigable without undue damage to land or to carriers' livelihoods. *(18)*

4

The Landowners' Battle Against the 'Act'

The final attempt to obtain Parliamentary approval for making the River Derwent navigable (from the Trent to Derby town) began in the late Autumn of 1719. This time the local landowners, organised mainly by Robert Wilmot, junior, of Osmaston who owned lands in Weston on Trent and on the banks of the Derwent, were united in their opposition. Wilmot was first alerted to the danger by his distant cousin Robert Holden (a barrister) who had been approached by Nottingham Corporation and reported discussions he had with Lord Chesterfield at Bretby. Robert Wilmot then entered into correspondence with as many of the aristocracy as he thought would be sympathetic to his cause. He also wrote to some members of the clergy who, however, tended to be very non-committal in their replies. Many of the replies can be seen in the Derbyshire Record Office, Matlock, and give an interesting account of the fight against the Bill as well as many anecdotes of life in those times for the 'landed gentry'. For instance a letter from Sir John Harpur's agent at Calke ends 'be pleased to let Mr. Ed. Wilmot know Sr. John hunts tomorrow on Swarson [Swarkestone] Side'. Another letter gives details of a litter of King Charles Spaniels (very fashionable at that time). There is also a graphic account of an attempted armed robbery in London 'thay shot of a pistell we suppose intending to shoot my Br. [brother] but as providence wod have it onely shot one of the horses ... thease thing keeps us women at home ...'! *(19)*

During this time there are also reports that indicate some underhand work. In order to get signatures on petitions in favour of the Derwent Navigation 'the Gentlemen at Derby have sent their Agents, not onely to your Tenants but to several Great and other Towns to gain Petitions; they go to an Ale—House there, and Pick up all the Scoundrells they can, and get some, that can write, to set their Hands to em, and they Sign, for the rest, themselves ...'. Derby had the support of their two Members of Parliament (Rt. Hon. James Cavendish and Sir William Stanhope), Sir Thomas Parker (by 1719, the Chancellor) and the Duke of Devonshire; most of the Whig Lords, the Scottish Lords and all but four of the Bishops in the House of Lords eventually voted in favour of the Bill. This appears to have been the result of intensive lobbying by the Chancellor and the Duke of Devonshire. *(20)*

Until the New Year of 1720, the local landowners did not believe that this Navigation Bill would progress any further than had its predecessors, but by

REASONS

Against making the River Derwent, *in the County of* Derby, *Navigable.*

First,   HERE is no Common Cart-Bridge over the River, *Derwent* below *Derby,* but many Fords, being High-ways through which Carts and Carriages daily, and Mill-Stones frequently pass. Now by making the River Navigable, all the Fords will be made unpassable, and the High-ways obstructed, and consequently all Commerce and Communications of the Inhabitants of the one side of the River, with those of the other, will be lost; and particularly the Carriage of Coal in the Summer-time over the River, (the Inhabitants on one side of the River being supply'd with Coals from the other side) will totally be lost, to the irreparable Damage of the Country thereabouts.

Secondly,   Upon this River are divers Corn-Mills and Fulling-Mills, the working of which this intended Navigation will frequently, if not altogether interrupt; and also will endanger the Breaking the Wears which turn the Water to the Mills, to the great Damage of the Country.

Thirdly,   This River of *Derwent* is very rapid, and has many quick and sudden Windings, and by reason thereof, in a very extraordinary manner, wears and washes away the Banks on each side; insomuch that the Land-Owners are forced to make Water-Works or Floitering, at very great Expence, against the Violence of the Stream of the River, for the Defence of their Lands, that is worth 40 or 50 s. per Acre. And if the Undertakers of this intended Navigation have Authority to cut the Banks of the River, and remove all Trees, Roots, Gravel-Beds, and other Impediments, that may in any wise hinder the Navigation either in Sailing, or Haling of Boats with Horses, Men, or otherwise, as by the Bill is proposed; then it will be in the Power of such Undertakers to cut and destroy such Floitering or Water-Works at their Will and Pleasure; and the Damage the Land-Owners may sustain thereby will be very difficult, if not impossible, to discover and ascertain. But the Inconvenience of this Navigation will not end here; for as it is endeavoured by the Bill to have a Power to make New Cuts or Passages for Water, through the Lands adjoining to or lying near the said River: And as the Navigators of *Derby* did heretofore employ Mr. *George Sorocold,* a very able and experienced Person in such kind of Works, to view and survey the River, in order for making the same Navigable, he took a Level of the River, and found the Fall of Water to be Fifty four Foot from the Town of *Derby* to the Place where the same falleth into the River *Trent,* and Map'd and drew out how and in what Manner the Navigation could only be effected; and he reported that it was impracticable ever to carry on the Navigation up the Old Channel of the River, but that several New Cuts must of Necessity be made through the Lands adjoining to and lying near the River; some of which Cuts, according to the Plan he drew thereof, would be upwards of half a Mile, and others upwards of a Mile in Length. Now in case the Land-Owners should have their Estates cut in sunder and divided, there would be no coming to the Land of both sides such Cuts, without the Assistance of Horse, and in some Places Cart-Bridges, the Building and Continuing of which must be an unspeakable Charge to the Proprietors of the Lands, besides all other Inconveniences that must unavoidably attend their Estates being so divided, and this intended Navigation. And it must seem very hard in Matters of such Owners are to receive for the Damage they shall sustain thereby, as by the Bill it is proposed *[...] other People* should be Arbiters of the Satisfaction such Land-

Fourthly,   If the *Derby* Navigators shall [...]

12 *Part of the document "Reasons Against making the River Derwent, in the County of Derby, Navigable". Derbyshire Record Office, D 3155/WH 2224. Reproduced by permission of the Education Officer (Archives).*

January they were getting concerned and the letter writing began in earnest. Robert Wilmot, junior, wrote to Lord Gower, Lord Pagett, Lord Ferrers, Lord Strafford, the Duke of Chandos (son-in-law of Francis Willoughby of Wollaton), Lord Scarsdale and the Earl of Chesterfield, also various Bishops. His wife (although reported in her daughter's letters, to hate writing) wrote to Lady Arran (who promised to talk to as many of her friends as possible) and other Bishops. Robert's father, Robert senior, had many friends who were still Members of Parliament, or maintained links with both Houses of Parliament, his son made use of these contacts to the full. The Wilmot family were also very well connected through marriage, with the medical, legal and political circles of London, and again Robert used all of these. *(21)*

In addition to all these influential opponents, many petitions were presented to Parliament opposing the Bill (see page 31). They included:- one from the 'Captains, Masters, Mates and Owners of Ships and Keels, Ropemakers, Sailmakers, mariners and other inhabitants of West and East Stockwith, Misterton, Kynnor Ferry & Butterwich'! However the Bill was passed by the House of Commons in February 1720, given the title of an Act and passed to the House of Lords. There various petitioners or their representatives were 'examined at the Barr of the House' and the opposers thought they had put forward a very good case. They were, however, disappointed not to have the support of Leonard Fosbrooke who they had hoped would speak against the Act at the Bar. It seems they continued to believe that Fosbrooke and Thomas Coke were with them, even though 'I am informed the Vice Chamberlaine [Coke] is about agreeing with the Derby Navigators, not to oppose the Bill, in case they will uphold his ferry at Wilden, and allow him to navigate on Vessels on the River Derwent toll free; which if true I doubt will be a blow to our Interest and deprive us of Mr. Fosbrooke's Evidence ...' (a solicitor's letter five days previous). This shows how well both Thomas Coke and Leonard Fosbrooke kept the secret of their change of heart, and what a blow it was to the opposers. *(22)*

Lobbying grew more intense when the Act proceeded to the House of Lords. Lord Chesterfield writes: 'I have writ to many Gentlemen ...'; and, from a legal friend, 'I have taken care to give his Grace [the Duke of Kingston] our Reasons, and also the Dukes of Rutland and Newcastle, I have given Reasons also to Lords Cooper, Trevor, Scarsdale, and the Bishop of Gloucester and Lord Gore ...'. However he continued 'had spoke to severall of the Scotch Lords, who were engaged by Lord Stanhope,' and that he doubted that 'if Lord Stanhope and Sunderland were zealous for the Bill, they would make too strong an Interest for us to oppose ... Lord Cooper ... who in opposicon to Ld. Chancellor may do us great service, this Bill being his [the Chancellor's] Creation ...'. Thus the opposing lines were drawn up. Lord Stanhope and the Chancellor - both local men and the originators of the Bill - had the backing of most of the Whig Lords, all the Scottish Lords and many of the Clergy, while the opposers to the Bill had most of the Tory Lords and as many more members of the Upper House as they could muster. To the great chagrin of the opposers the Act was passed by Parliament in March 1720. *(23)*

13 *(facing page) Letter from Lord Chesterfield to Robert Wilmot. Derbyshire Record Office, D 3155/WH 2270. Reproduced by permission of the Education Officer (Archives).*

Feb the 26 1719

Sr

I am to thank you for the favor of
sending your own servant with my
Petition to London and wish it may
do any good. But in good truth, Earl
Stanhope, and the Chancellor, have
(to say no worse) so many Friends in
the House of Lords, that We may with
reason expect the worst. I am inform'd
(and from the best hands) that it was
by their means, the Bill had so quick
a dispatch in the House of Commons
and with very little opposition. I can
assure you money was not wanting to
carry that Babe of Grace (I mean the
Bill) through that House, and which
puts me in mind of an exclamation
of Virgils ——

Auri sacra fames, quid non mortalia
pectora coges?

When your servant comes back from London I desire the
favor of you to send him to me, and by which you will oblige

Sr your assure Friend.
Chesterfield.

The correspondence during this time includes a number of letters from Lord Chesterfield to Robert Wilmot, junior. Lord Chesterfield wrote of his 'old friend' Robert's father and took an interest in the son and his family, as well as opposing the Bill. Lord Chesterfield's letters show the family flair for writing 'I am much consern'd at the Account you send me of my old Friend your Father by which I doubt he cant last long, and when he is gone, the best tribute I can pay to his honest memory, is to show my civilities to you who are to supply his place'; and 'you may expect now to find the Projectors and Stock Jobbers, very prou'd and domenering. Because tis the nature of mean, base spirits, to be proud, haughty, sawsey and insolent in prosperity, as much as they are low, and dijected in adversity ...'. Later he wrote: 'Adieu Liberty, and Property; it is vain to say any more ...'. In another letter he said: 'I am inform'd (and from the best hands) that it was by their [Earl Stanhope and the Chancellor] means, the Bill had so quick a dispatch in the House of Commons. I can assure you money was not wanting to carry that Babe of Grace (I mean the Bill) through that House ...' following which is a quotation from Virgil about the 'accursed greed for money!' - he often included a Latin quotation in his letters (see page 33). Later, when all seemed lost he wrote 'what a fine Age We live in, and what a happy people We are grown, when because a Thing is popular, it shall take place of Justice's ... At this rate, if a Gentleman chance to be obnoxious to a Corporation Town it may be a very popular thing to have him hang'd, or nockt on the head by the Mob's and then Factum valet, as the Judges cry in Westminster Hall when they have hang'd a man unjustly'. Finally 'I am inform'd ... that the Stock Jobbers, and those fellows at Derby, have a most virulent spleen against you in particular, and that they are determined ... to do your Land and Estate all the mischief they can ... take what precautions you are able against the designs of such wicked Rogues, who are as void of honour, and honesty, as they are of learning, or good manners ...'. *(24)*

Robert had already received an anonymous threat in the form of an invitation, '... you will be seranaded with a Noble Consort of Musick when you come to town ... 36 letters lately, with more before, deserves ye most venoration, ye Musick will be cleever & hacket, frying pan drums, Bulk Knockers, dulsemor and Belloss, Cay & Tonges ... [after which] ... ye Company will give ye hum, ye his & ye clap ...'! It must be remembered that all post, to and from London in particular, went via Wilden Ferry and Fosbrooke was on the side of the proposed Derby Navigators. He had already admitted, in letters to Thomas Coke, to a knowledge of the contents of the post bags, so he must have kept a tally of Robert Wilmot's letters, except for the local ones which were hand-delivered by servants. This letter has other overtones, as this type of 'musick' was played outside houses where villagers knew, or suspected, an affair or 'cuckoldry' was going on, hence the term 'face the music'. *(25)*

5

After the Navigation Act, to the Derby Canal Act

The 'Act for making the River Darwent in the County of Derby Navigable' (see page 36) listed the 'Undertakers' who were, at their own expense, to make the river navigable from its mouth to Derby, as William Woolley, Thomas Gisborne, Benjamin Blundell junior, Thomas Rivet, Abraham Crompton, John Chambers, Francis Cockayne, Robert Wagstaffe, Samuel Fox and Samuel Shepperdson (three of these had been mayors of Derby during the previous nine years) their Heirs and Assigns. It was to be 'navigable and passable with and for Barges, Boats, Keels, Lighters and other Vessels'. The route was to be 'from the Mouth or end of the said River, where the said River doth run or fall into the River of Trent to the Town of Derby up the Holmes Mill Fleam, and so into the Morledge'. *(26)*

The Undertakers were allowed to 'cleanse, scour, open and enlarge or straiten the same River and dig or cut the Banks . . . make new or larger Cuts or Trenches or Passages for Water . . . if necessity requires, to remove and take away all Trees, Roots, Gravel Beds . . . which may . . . hinder Navigation . . . to Build erect, set up and make . . . any such Locks, Wears, Turnpikes, pens for Water, Wharfs, Cranes, Warehouses and other things proper and convenient for such intended Navigation . . . alter, repair and amend the same . . .'. They were to have free access to all parts of the river for their construction work, repair, navigation etc. However they must come to an agreement with the landowners and if there were any problems they should obtain an 'Order' from the board of 'Commissioners'. The Act lists these Commissioners (133 in all) who would oversee the works and mediate in any disputes. This list includes all the local landowners who had opposed the Bill, as well as those in favour, for example two sons of the Duke of Devonshire, the Marquis of Granby (son of the Duke of Rutland), Lord Chesterfield's son, Thomas Coke, Sir George Parker, and members of the local families of Harpur, Coke, Curzon, Stanhope, Wilmot, Burdett, Holden, Mundy, Lowe, and Pole; the Mayor, Aldermen and Recorder of Derby; two Doctors of Divinity; many representatives of commercial interests in the town; and various others including Leonard Fosbrooke. Any nine of the Commissioners could mediate between the Undertakers and landowners, fix payments or compensation, impose fines, issue warrants for arrest or summon to the Court anyone preventing work progressing. Anyone summoned to Court was to be tried by a Jury of 12 independent men who would then advise the

An Act for making the River Darwent in the County of Derby Navigable. — 6ᵗʰ Geo: 1ˢᵗ Chap: 27ᵗʰ 1719.

Whereas the making the River Darwent in the County of Derby Navigable will be of great Advantage to the public as well as to the several and respective Traders and Dealers in Lead, Butter, Cheese, Malt, Marble, Grindstones, Scythe stones, Iron, Timber and other the Commodities and Manufactures of the said County of Derby and Places adjacent, by a much cheaper and easier Conveyance than at present by Land Carriage; and will also tend very much to the preserving of the Roads thereabouts, which at some seasons of the year are almost impassable: May it therefore please You most excellent Majesty, that it may be enacted; and be it enacted by the Kings most excellent Majesty, by and with the advice and Consent of the Lords Spiritual and Temporal, and Commons in this present Parliament assembled, and by the authority of the same, That William Woolley, Thomas Gisborne, Benjamin Blundell Jun; Thomas Rivett, Esquires, Abraham Crompton, John Chambers, Francis Cokayne, Robert Wagstaffe, Samuel Fox and Samuel Shepperdson, Gentlemen their Heirs and Assigns, for the general᷃ of all his Majestys Subjects, by themselves, their Deputies, Agents, Officers, Workmen and Servants are hereby impowered and Authorized, and shall have full power & Authori;

Undertakers impowered at their own expence to make the Derwent Navigable from the Mouth of the River to Derby.

Commissioners of the fine to be imposed, or would recommend imprisonment. It should however be noted that since all the landowners likely to be involved were Commissioners, the fines etc. were quite likely to be biased in their favour - there is no mention of the nine Commissioners being disinterested parties! The Commissioners could impose fines for damage to land or property during construction, navigation, or due to flooding where any newly constructed banks had not been sufficiently strong to hold the water (a particular worry of Lord Chesterfield who owned land at Draycott which could be subject to flooding). The local Constable could be called upon to 'levy such Damages, Costs and Charges . . . by Distress and Sale of all or any of the Undertakers Goods and Chattels . . .' or the Undertakers after trial by Jury, could be committed 'to the Common Goal of the County of Derby there to remain without Bail or Mainprize, until Payment as aforesaid'.

The Undertakers could also set up 'Winches and other Engines' to assist the 'Strength of Men, Horses or other Beasts' in haling [hauling] vessels up the river, but neither the Undertakers, boatmen or beasts were to 'meddle' with any land whilst construction was in process until agreement had been reached and compensation had been paid. The exception to this was for surveying, marking and laying out of the ground. If the water level was to be raised above its normal by construction of a 'Wear or Dam', the banks were to be raised and strengthened to prevent flooding. All fences, gates, bridges, fords, fisheries etc. were to be preserved and the Undertakers were to construct bridges at their own expense if any part of a person's land became inaccessible by other means due to the river work. The working of mills was not to be disturbed. The Masters and Owners were to be responsible for any damage done by their vessels by payment of a fine, with the ultimate threat of the 'Common Goal'.

Construction of 'Wharfs in or near the Holmes Mill Fleam or Race, or in the Morledge adjoining thereunto, for the convenient lading or unlading of Goods . . .' was to be undertaken with all possible speed 'which said Wharfs . . . shall be adjudged, deemed and taken to be Public'. The wharfage fee was not to exceed two pence per ton, the rates for carriage of goods to or from Derby were not to exceed one shilling per ton with appropriate decreases for smaller amounts or distances. There was to be no extra charge for the occupiers of the boats. Owners of land adjacent to the river had the right to use their own boats on the river for pleasure or for carrying manure, 'Corn in the Straw, Hay and other produce of the Lands' free of charge provided they did not carry any other produce.

14 *(facing page) Part of a contemporary transcript of the Act for making the River Derwent Navigable. Derbyshire Record Office, D 3155/WH 2207. Reproduced by permission of the Education Officer (Archives).*

Work progressed rapidly. Sorocold's original ideas to straighten the river by long cuts, with locks, were not carried out since they would be too time consuming. Wharves were rapidly built, so that on January 17th 1721 - only ten months after the passing of the Act - the first boat to navigate the river arrived in Derby. This was joyfully reported in the *Derby Postman* the following day:- 'Yesterday arrived here a Boat laden with Dale-Boards, Tobacco, Fish and other Merchandises Etc. which being the first fruits of a Bill that passed the last Sessions of Parliament . . . was received with Ringing of Bells and other Demonstrations of Joy ... met by some Hundreds of People, who all proclaim'd their Satisfaction ... by loud Huzza's ... Trumpets, Drums and other sorts of Musick ...'. The water was said to be 'so high' [the January floods] that the boat easily navigated the mill-fleam and went 'a considerable way into Town'. The newspaper reported that another boat was on the way up-river and that the first boat returned downstream with a cargo of lead. It was expected that trade would increase as the weather improved in the spring. *(27)*

At this time all river boats, although supplied with a sail which could be used when the wind was favourable, were 'haled' [hauled] by teams of 'boatmen'. These teams could number twenty men or more when hauling upstream against a strong current, but might be reduced to about two men for the downstream journey. The boatmen were known as very rough and uncouth 'idle dissolute Fellows' who regularly poached landowner's game and fish, but the suggestion of replacing them with horses was quite strongly opposed by the same landowners! Use of 'horses or other beasts' was not allowed until various Acts of Parliament in the late 1700s; for example the relevant Act for the River Trent was dated 1783. It caused considerable hardship in the villages along the Trent valley when this source of employment for the men ceased to be available. *(28)*

On January 19th 1721 the *Derby Postman* printed a poem written by Robert Bateman (the Mayor at the time was Hugh Bateman - a relative perhaps?). The first few lines may give some indication of the intensity of public feeling at the time against Nottingham, for its opposition to the River Derwent navigation. It is entitled - *'Choak-Pear for Nottingham, etc.'*

'When Derby's Derwent Gain doth Inchoate,
Then Nottingham may wag its broken Pate,
Gainst whom it hath its Malice so defus'd,
By them as just, the Serpents Head is bruis'd;
And as their Plea was much for th'Carriers good,
They must dissemble or contribute Food;
But 'tis in doubt, their Goodness is in thrawl,
To th'Evil Spirit that obsessed Saul'. *(29)*

In 1734 a slitting mill was built by William Evans on the Holmes. This mill later passed into the hands of Thomas Evans (unrelated except that he married William's heiress), who was the owner of lead mines at Bonsall, a co-partner in the Crompton, Evans Bank of Derby and towards the end of the century was the builder (with his sons) of a cotton spinning mill, paper mill, the weir, toll bridge and mill workers' community at Darley Abbey. He had acquired the Darley Abbey site when the previous owner was made bankrupt.

Evans' slitting mill (worked by a water wheel) prepared iron for various purposes and provided a useful source of employment in the town. Ironstone was available from east Derbyshire and small smelters were producing wrought iron before Hurt's smelting works at Alderwasley expanded and furnaces were developed at Morley Park, south of Heage. In Evans' mill wrought iron was rolled into sheets, whilst the power from the same water

15 *Present day Darley Mills, toll bridge and weir.*

wheel operated cutting rollers so that strips of metal were produced. These would be used for articles such as horse shoes, nails or wire depending on thickness. Iron wire was needed at this time for making wire sieves (eg. those used by lead miners), wool cards (for 'carding' raw wool, etc.) and knitting needles. These products were easily exported from the town via the river, instead of the laborious road transport previously used.

This mill was followed three years later, by another Evans mill this time for the smelting, rolling and working of copper. Evans probably had connections in Wales where copper was mined, but copper had also been mined at Ecton since the 1600s. In the late 1730s the mine, whose mineral rights were owned by successive Dukes of Devonshire until the early 19th century, was leased and worked by John Gilbert, who owned Locko Park before the Lowe family bought it in 1747. He transported the copper by pack horse to be smelted at Denby, so this was probably the main source of Evans' copper. Also the Duke of Devonshire had a contract with the navy to provide the copper for sheathing of ships' hulls. This was to reduce worm and barnacle growth, but eventually resulted in corrosion of the iron rudder fittings, an inexplicable result then, but now known to be due to electrolytic reaction between the two metals.

The first silk mill in Derby had been built in 1702 by Thomas Cotchett on the Bye Flatt, a small islet by the west bank of the river close to the site of corn mills and the water wheel which was part of Derby's water supply. Cotchett's mill was a three-storey building with a 13½ ft. diameter water wheel. The engineer for this factory was George Sorocold and he was employed as engineer again when Thomas Lombe of London built a five-storey mill and installed Italian inspired machinery in 1717/1722. Thus the famous Lombe

Silk Mill was in full operation by the time the river was opened for navigation so could take advantage of the improved transport and communication this provided. The present building (appropriately now the Industrial Museum) is of a more recent construction, only three storeys high with a modified tower. The bridge and mill race have gone, an electricity sub-station standing in their position. The old Silk Mill gates, a Robert Bakewell masterpiece now restored, are back close to their original position (for River Derwent before and after the 1720 Act, see maps pages 19 and 41).

In 1743 the 'Derby Navigators' under the leadership of Sir Thomas Gisborne (Mayor of Derby in 1712) leased Wilden Ferry from George Lewis Coke (Thomas Coke's bachelor son and heir, who died in 1750), together with the fishery, ferry house, some meadow land and an osier bed. This gave them control over both road and river transport south from Derby. Thus ended Leonard Fosbrooke's monopoly of transport on road and river in the area. *(30)*

The mills at Borrowash and Wilne, both owned by the Stanhopes of Elvaston, continued to function. Their weirs were bypassed by cuts and locks which allowed passage of boats without too much loss of water for the mill. They both had quite a diverse usage, including corn milling, fulling of cloth, sheet lead rolling, cotton spinning and dyeing. A clause was always included in the lease stating that the owner would give three days notice to the miller, of diversion of the river for repair of locks or weirs.

16 *Derby Silk Mill, now the Industrial Museum.*

Although the roads from Derby to Manchester and Sheffield (in common with many others between 1720 and 1758) were successfully turnpiked, delays at Wilden Ferry caused problems and congestion on the section of the turnpike south towards Leicester and London. As a result of this in December 1757 Thomas Coke's son-in-law, Sir Matthew Lamb, obtained an Act of Parliament to build a bridge over the River Trent and close the ferry. The 'Derby Navigators' had to relinquish their lease of the ferry to Sir Matthew Lamb on 6th April 1758, being paid £520.5.0d for the purchase of the rest of the lease. Wilden Ferry was to continue until the bridge was built but was to be run by the Trustees of the bridge who were to pay Sir Matthew Lamb £150 per annum as recompense for loss of his ferry. After the bridge was built the ferry was to cease, unless needed due to accidents to the structure. The Duke of Devonshire was to be paid £278 per annum out of the bridge tolls until he had been repaid the full £3333 which he put up for the construction. In his honour the bridge was named 'Cavendish Bridge'. This bridge stood until the winter

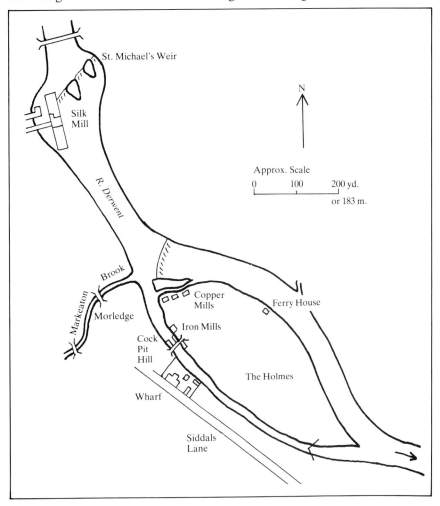

17 *Derby and the River Derwent, about 1740.*

storms of 1947 caused its collapse; its place was taken by a temporary Bailey Bridge which was eventually superseded by the present bridge in 1956. At the same time the opportunity was taken to straighten out the A6 so that it now bypasses Cavendish village. *(31)*

Similar conditions on tolls were included in the Act of Parliament (in 1788) which authorised the construction of a bridge to replace the ferry at Sawley (the Harrington Bridge). These payments went to Lord Harrington and Sir Henry Harpur. In 1882 the trustees of the two bridges were combined and in 1893-6 the two bridges and Willington Bridge were freed of tolls and taken over by the respective County Councils. The accumulated tolls were used to finance the building of a bridge over the River Derwent at Borrowash. *(32)*

On 30th December 1765 a preliminary meeting was held at Wolseley Bridge (near Stafford) to agree an application to Parliament to construct a navigable canal between '... the River Trent at or near Wilden Ferry, in the County of Derby, to the River Mersey'. This was not the first time the suggestion of a canal had been made, many ideas had already been put forward, but this was the beginning of the final successful application. The meeting was reported to Lord Uxbridge who owned a great deal of land in Burton upon Trent and the surrounding areas, by his agent. Lord Uxbridge became the landowner most affected by the Grand Trunk, or Trent and Mersey, Canal when finally construction commenced in June 1766. Although the Trent and Mersey Canal does not affect the River Derwent (it finally joined the River Trent at the confluence between the Rivers Derwent and Trent), it passed through Willington which at the time was much more accessible to Derby than Wilden Ferry. This meant that traffic on the River Derwent and road traffic from Wilden Ferry to Derby could be considerably affected by the proximity of the new canal.

River traffic was often disrupted by the vagaries of the climate, floods in winter and drought in summer (or even just low water levels) making navigation on both the Rivers Derwent and Trent uncertain. The *Derby Mercury* of 23rd January 1767 reported that '... navigation upon the Rivers Trent and Derwent being entirely stopped on account of the present frost and the boatmen out of Employ . . .', twenty of the men showed their strength and stamina by drawing a waggon of coals weighing 73cwt. from Aston on Trent to Derby, where they had a collection, and then hauled the waggon back to Aston. *(33)*

The uncertainty of river levels and greater dependability of canal transport demonstrated by the Trent and Mersey and other canals, encouraged a group calling themselves the 'Derby Committee' to begin consultations with Benjamin Outram, with a view to the construction of a Derby Canal connecting with the Grand Trunk system. In 1793 they produced an interesting document and map showing a proposed canal from Swarkestone Lock on the Trent and Mersey to Derby, another from the Erewash Canal near 'Sandy-acre' Lock through Borrowash to Derby, these two were to join north of the River Derwent and then a branch would continue north to join a tramway from 'Smalley Mill' and 'Smithey Houses', at Little Eaton. This rivalled a proposal from the Grand Trunk Canal Company, who suggested one canal from Moorside, Aston on Trent, via Boulton to Derby and a small connection between the Erewash Canal at Long Eaton and the Grand Trunk at Great Wilne. This connection, being a continuation of the Nottingham to Erewash Canal, cut out the River Trent navigation between Nottingham and Shardlow which was still variable due to shoals and weather conditions (see map, page 44). William Jessop was asked to comment on the two rival schemes and, not surprisingly since they were business partners, reported at length in favour of Outram's plans. He made a few recommendations such as:-

1. that the line north of Swarkestone should pass across the south-east of Sinfin Moor (rather than close to Chellaston), because there was 'better Ground for the Purpose . . .',

2. that instead of joining the Grand Trunk Canal at Cuttle Bridge a junction above Swarkestone Lock would be more advisable. This should be followed by a descent of three locks to the River Trent at a point 'about twelve Chains . . .' further up the Grand Trunk,

3. that the proposed junctions would be more favourable to the Grand Trunk Canal Committee than an aqueduct over, which 'would have a very unfriendly Appearance'.

He was quite definitely in favour of the proposed crossing of the River Derwent in Derby and of the canal to Little Eaton with tramway extensions to Smithy Houses and Smalley Mills for the colliery trade. *(34)*

The Derby Canal Act was passed in 1793, the engineer was Benjamin Outram and construction was soon under way, being fully completed on 30th June 1796 although the Little Eaton and Sandiacre branches were opened in 1795. The canal from Derby to Swarkestone continued across the Trent and Mersey Canal as suggested, with a link to the River Trent via a flight of locks. In order to use this boats had to pay a considerable toll to the Trent and Mersey Canal Company and consequently it was little used. It soon fell into disuse and by 1837 had been drained and is now used as farmland. Nevertheless the line of it can still be discerned in parts of Swarkestone.

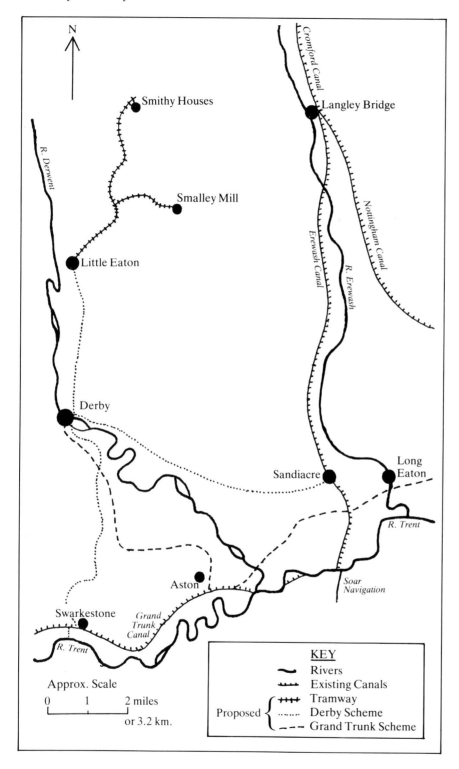

N

19 *Suggestions for the proposed Derby Canal, 1793.*

Smithy Houses

Smalley Mill

R. Derwent

Cromford Canal

Langley Bridge

Nottingham Canal

Erewash Canal

R. Erewash

Little Eaton

Derby

Sandiacre

Long Eaton

R. Trent

Soar Navigation

Aston

Swarkestone

Grand Trunk Canal

R. Trent

Approx. Scale

0   1   2 miles

or 3.2 km.

KEY

〰 Rivers

Existing Canals

Proposed {
+++ Tramway
.... Derby Scheme
--- Grand Trunk Scheme

20 *Junction of the Derby and Erewash Canals at Sandiacre, the Derby Canal entrance is now blocked.*

It is interesting to note that there was comparatively little opposition to the proposed Derby Canal. The Derwent River Navigation had been useful initially but could not cope with the increase of trade which it was partially instrumental in generating. It suffered from great variations in river level which often prevented carriage of goods for many days and it was a very circuitous route since Sorocold's suggestions to bypass the large meanders were not followed. The proposed canal was both direct and would not be affected by lack of water in the same way. The main problems with canals had been found to be icing in winter (which was unavoidable) and lack of water in canals which had to mount hills via 'staircases' of locks. Derby's proposed canal had few locks being mostly on the level, but still had water supply problems. The hills were avoided by constructing a tramway. The descendants of many of the landowners who had opposed the river navigation were in favour of the canal. Many canals had been built, 'Canal Fever' was rife, large profits were promised and expected. Sir Robert Wilmot in particular was favourably inclined - and the canal was to pass mainly through his land.

6

The Finale

The two rival navigation companies seem to have assumed at first that they would be able to co-exist even though traffic on the river had decreased considerably since the opening of the Trent and Mersey Canal, turnpiking of the Derby to London road via Shardlow and building of Cavendish Bridge. However even before construction was complete, the canal company took a one year lease on 'all Locks, Bridges, Wharfs, Warehouses, Buildings, Yards, Lands ... and other works' of the River Derwent Navigation. In theory the river navigation was not interrupted immediately but it can be assumed that the canal company intended to close down their rival; and it was not long before the river company sold out to the canal company. Various authorities state the figure of £3996 as being paid, but Glover in his *History and Gazetteer of the County of Derby* states that 'the Derby Canal Company paid £40,000 as compensation to the members of the Derwent Navigation which the canal had rendered useless ...', so they did not get away with it too lightly! *(35)*

The Derby Canal is like an upturned 'Y' in shape with the pivot in Derby centre. One branch went to Swarkestone and the 'leg' supplied Little Eaton, the other branch went at first parallel to the Nottingham Road and then across

21 *The junction of the Derby and Trent & Mersey Canals at Swarkestone, showing the Toll House for Derby Canal traffic.*

22 *(above) Shelton Lock, Derby Canal, from a painting by Jean Goodwin. (Photograph supplied by John Heath).*

23 *(left) Shelton Lock today. The stonework in the foreground was part of the lock.*

24 *The cast iron aqueduct which carried Derby canal across the Markeaton Brook/Holmes Mill Fleam. (Photograph supplied by John Heath).*

25 *Long Bridge, Derby Canal, demolished in 1959. (Photograph supplied by Frank Rodgers).*

country to a junction with the Erewash Canal at Sandiacre Lock (see picture, page 45). Travelling via these two canals eliminated much of the River Trent navigation from Nottingham especially when the Nottingham Canal (1796), Beeston Canal (1795) and the Cranfleet Cut had been made. This route also nearly sounded the 'death-knell' of the Trent and Mersey Canal as wide boats could pass up the Erewash (1779) and then Cromford (1792) Canals, via the Cromford and High Peak Railway (opened full length 1831) to the Peak Forest Canal (1800) and so to Manchester, all these canals being 'wide'. The Trent and Mersey route necessitated trans-shipping to narrow boats for the passage from Horninglow Basin, Burton upon Trent, to Middlewich. In this section the canal locks were only constructed seven feet wide. It is generally considered that Brindley designed the narrow section of the canal to reduce expenditure on construction of both the canal itself and the Harecastle tunnel, and to save water, but it also restricted use.

The Derby Canal ran from Swarkestone (see picture, page 46) towards the town via Shelton Lock (see pictures, page 47) and Wilmorton, then along beside the Holmes Mill Fleam and across it by a cast iron aqueduct. It then cut across the Holmes towards the River Derwent. This aqueduct is believed to be the first made in cast iron in the country and predates the bigger one on the Shrewsbury Canal (at Longdon on Tern) by about a month. It was made by the Butterley Company in five sections each six feet deep, eight feet long at the top and nine feet at the bottom, of overall 2 inch thick metal. These sections were bolted together in situ. Benjamin Outram and William Jessop were partners in the Butterley Company. In order to cross the river a narrow wooden bridge - the 'Long Bridge' -was constructed. The horses walked over this bridge drawing the boats across on the upstream side. Damage to the bridge was prevented by a thick wooden 'bumper rail' fixed on the upstream side of the supports. The bridge was often damaged by debris carried by flood waters, however it remained until declared unsafe in 1950 and was demolished in 1959.

Various town maps of the time although not of the standard of present day Ordnance Survey maps, give a good idea of developments resulting from the canal. The area of the Holmes and Morledge went through considerable changes, as can be seen from the accompanying sketch maps (see page 50). The single large weir on the Derwent which had effectively prevented navigation any higher up the river, became two weirs when a fresh one was constructed just downstream of the Long Bridge. This made the crossing of canal boats much easier by smoothing out the water flow. Wharves and warehouses were built, as was a 'weighing house' - the fore-runner of a public weighbridge. Elaborate basins and wharves were constructed by companies so that loading and unloading of boats could continue unaffected by canal traffic.

In addition to the canal connection with the River Trent, the Derby Canal Act stated that, should the owner [Lord Stamford] of the 'Limeworks at Breedon ...' desire to construct a canal or railway from the quarry to the River Trent at Weston Cliff, the proprietors of the Derby Canal were to

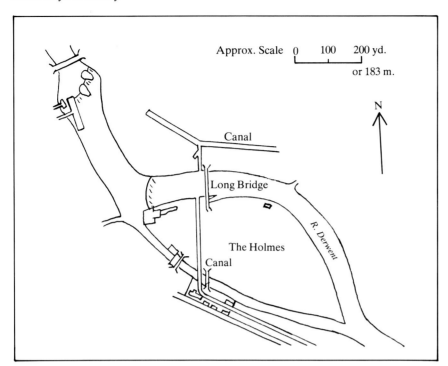

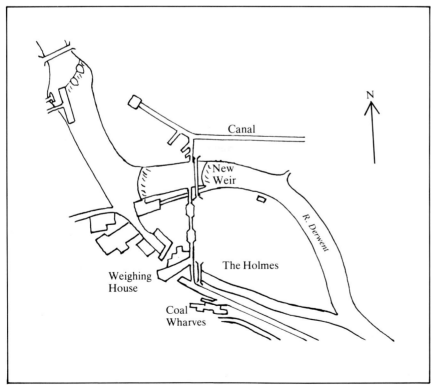

26 *Derby Canal developments, 1806 (top) and 1819.*

construct a connection between the river and the Trent and Mersey Canal. This was to take the same form as the connection at Swarkestone, to have the same restrictions on water use and the same high tolls as applied at Swarkestone. This connection was never made, Breedon Cloud Quarry being eventually linked by rail to the south to join the Burton upon Trent to Leicester railway. The railway which eventually passed close to Breedon and north via Melbourne to the Trent Valley main line was a much later construction. *(36)*

Another section of the Act permitted construction of a 'railway' [often called a 'tramway', 'plateway' or, as is usual for this particular one, a 'gangway'] from the northern branch of the canal at Little Eaton (see picture, page 52) to 'Smithey Houses [near Denby] and Smalley Mills'. This was proposed by Outram as a convenient connection to collieries and the ironstone areas, over terrain where canal construction would be difficult and was greatly favoured by William Jessop in his 'Report to the . . . Subscribers to the intended Derby Canals'. One assumes that again, the Butterley Company would be involved in supplying the iron works for the gangway, but they did not supply the original rails which came from Joseph Butler of Wingerworth at ten guineas a ton. However, these were flawed and had to be replaced in 1800 by flanged rails. The Smithy Houses/Denby route proved very useful and was soon extended by branches to various collieries, eg.

27 *The wharfhouse at the junction of the Derby Canal and the Little Eaton Gangway. Stonework indicates the possible lines of the canal.*

Openwoodgate and Salterwood. The Smalley Mill branch is interesting. The Act states that 'Philip, Earl of Chesterfield . . . intends soon to open a colliery at or near Horsley . . .' and if he should require it, the Derby Canal Company were to build a rail or wagon way (not exceeding one mile in length) either branching from the railway to Smalley Mill or the one to Smithy Houses. Also Phillips, in his manual on *Inland Navigation 1805*, states that ' . . . the principal rail-way to Smithey houses is 4½ miles and to Smalley mills is 1¾ miles . . .'. The implication is that Smalley Mill was a stone or ironstone crushing mill. However these are the only references to a section of the gangway in the direction of Smalley Mill found to date. No remains seem to be visible and the writer has yet to find a map showing its route, apart from the map of 'proposals' prior to passing of the Act (see map, page 44). *(37)*

Eventually the Derby Canal also had a connection with the River Derwent just south of St. Mary's Bridge and above the St. Michael's weir. This weir was constructed to increase the depth of water for the Silk Mill water wheels and replaced the old 'Causey'. This connection was also allowed for in the Act and enabled boats to proceed up-river as far as Thomas Evans' mills at Darley

28 *Little Eaton Gangway/Derby Canal wharf. Loading the detachable part of a waggon onto a canal boat. (Photograph supplied by John Heath).*

Abbey. The Act also stated that cast iron pipes were to be laid in the bed of the weir to be constructed for the Long Bridge crossing of the river. These were to 'connect the waters of the south and north canals . . .'. This was presumably to prevent loss of water into the canal from the river, causing reduced water levels at the mills downstream.

The Derby Canal which remained privately owned until its final abandonment in 1964, was never a great financial success as were some other canals built during the 'Canal Fever' era. It had cost in the region of £100,000 to build, £10,000 above the amount allowed in the Act, and dividends were limited to a maximum of 8%. The high construction costs put a strain upon the resources of the Company; also one of the clauses in the Authorising Act stated that 5000 tons of coal were to be carried into Derby annually free of rates ' . . . for the use of the poor of that town'. Any surplus profit was to be set aside to form a £4000 emergency reserve, after which tolls etc. were to be lowered so that the 8% dividend was not exceeded. Thus although the canal was a steady if not sparkling success, the advantages to the town far exceeded the profit enjoyed by the subscribers.

29 *Derby Canal. A painting of the wharf at Cockpit Hill with Gandy's warehouse on the right. (Photograph supplied by John Heath).*

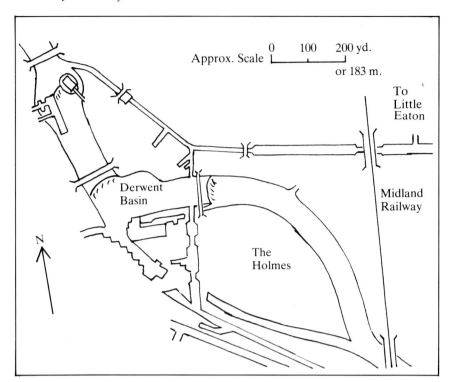

30 *Derby Canal developments, 1852 (top) and 1900.*

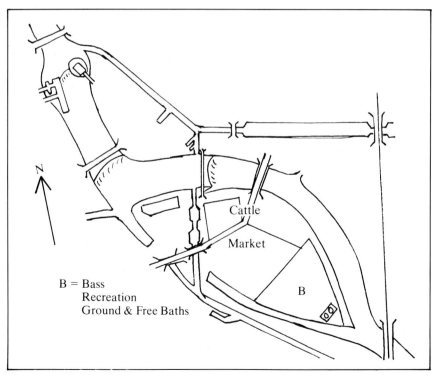

The social impact of the canal however, was considerable for it produced an even greater surge of industry into the town than did the River Derwent Navigation (see picture page 53). A steady industrialization of the Holmes, Morledge and Siddals areas of the town proceeded with frequent alterations and additions to existing wharves, warehouses and mills (see maps, opposite). This steady expansion continued until the 'Railway Age' began - this is generally regarded as commencing during the 1830s after the successful launch of the Liverpool and Manchester Railway. The Midland Counties Railway Act of 1836 proposed a connection between Derby, Nottingham, Leicester and Rugby. This Act had of course, been vigorously opposed by the canal companies, but 'Railway Fever' had replaced 'Canal Fever' and they were not successful in stopping the progress of the railways.

It is interesting here to note how river navigation was opposed by land carriers and land owners fearing loss of trade and land; canal building was opposed by river navigators and land owners fearing loss of trade and land; and finally railways were opposed by canal companies mainly, fearing loss of trade. Many land owners had by now become major shareholders in the railways, although some continued to oppose railway construction over their land. As a result of opposition most Railway Acts, like the preceding Canal and River Acts, allowed for compensation to be negotiated between the company involved, the land owner and the Commissioners or Proprietors. However, as with the River Derwent Act, most of the land owners involved were either on or connected with the controlling Board, so the compensation negotiated was often quite generous! Thus on the Board of Promoters of the Derby Canal, were Sir Robert Wilmot (grandson of Robert Wilmot, junior, the prime objector to the River Derwent Navigation - but who was also one of the Commissioners for the River Navigation), Charles Holden, and George Wheeldon, each of whom owned land destined to be cut for the canal.

Competition between the railways and the canals became a price war, cutting of carriage rates by each protagonist, which inevitably led to a reduction of profits and a decline in living standards for the canal carrier. This is generally regarded as the time when the whole family became nomadic, moved on to and worked the boats. Previously the boats were worked by a man and boy or two men, there being enough money for the family to remain land-dwellers.

The Derby Canal continued in operation well into the late 19th century, but by the early 1900s it was little used. The First World War resulted in a small increase in traffic but this declined in the 1920s so that by 1935 the canal was barely operational (see picture, page 56). Since it was a small undertaking and mainly derelict it was entirely overlooked in the nationalization of waterways into the British Transport Commission in 1948. This left the owners with a derelict canal on their hands. Having completely failed to sell their canal to the railways in the 1800s as did many canal companies ('if you can't beat them, join them!'), they found it necessary to sell off the land in the 1950s. This they did, selling small sections to industrial concerns so that very few canal remains can be seen in the centre of the city (see maps, page 58). The canal was finally

31 *(top left) Borrowash Lock, Derby Canal, showing in 1834 the lockhouse, built when the canal was re-routed as a result of construction of the Midland Counties railway line between Derby and Nottingham.*

32 *(bottom left) Borrowash Lock in the late 1940s.*

33 *(right) Borrowash Lock 1965.*

34 *(below) Sandiacre Lock, Derby Canal, after closure. Erewash Canal junction is beyond the bridge.*

(All photographs on this page supplied by John Heath).

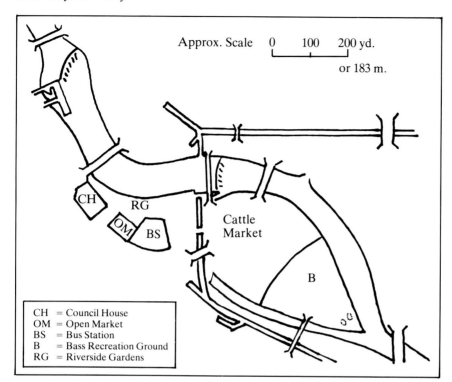

Approx. Scale   0   100   200 yd.

or 183 m.

CH = Council House
OM = Open Market
BS = Bus Station
B   = Bass Recreation Ground
RG = Riverside Gardens

35 *The decline of the Derby Canal, 1959 (top) and 1989.*

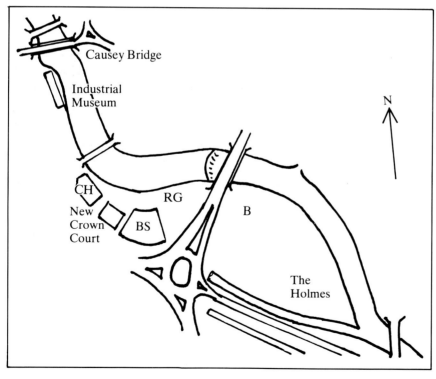

abandoned in 1964, the company entering into agreements with Derbyshire County Council and the Trent River Board. *(38)*

With the closure of the canal it appeared that all interest in water-borne transport and its riverside had ceased in Derby, the banks of the river and adjoining areas (with the exception of a small area of gardens in the city centre) generally became a 'dumping ground'. However in 1988 Derby City Council put forward 'Project Riverlife' which was intended to open up and develop the Derby riverside. By June 1989 the scheme was officially launched and was to involve developers, environmental groups and organisations (local, public and private) in an effort to revitalise the riverside aspect of Derby, particularly the areas to the south and south-east of the City. The aim was to improve access to the riverside, improve the river's visual quality as well as recreational use and to encourage improvement of their riverside frontage by organisations so endowed. The Project from its initiation received generous backing from Courtaulds Acetate and from Severn Trent Water. Derby City Council are now in partnership with Courtaulds Acetate, the Countryside Commission, the National Rivers Authority and English Nature who are contributing financial assistance as well as 'support and advice' to further 'Riverlife'. Improvements have been made and work continues, eventually the residents of Derby will be able to emulate their predecessors who, according to Woolley in 1712, used the Holmes for 'the most pleasant walk about the town . . .'. *(39)*

36 *The Riverlife Project, improvements near St. Mary's Bridge, Derby, note new footpath/cycleway, part of the proposed Little Eaton to Melbourne route.*

Bibliography

Manuscript Sources

Historical Manuscripts Commission, Cowper MSS, (1889), Vol 2.

Historical Manuscripts Commission, Middleton. MSS HMSO, (1911) ed. Stevenson. W.H., Nottingham Local Studies Library.

Catton Papers, Derbyshire Record Office, D.3155.

Harpur-Crewe Papers, Derbyshire Record Office, D.2375.

Lothian Papers, Melbourne Hall, X.94.

Official Publications

Acts of Parliament. Derbyshire Record Office.

Journals of the House of Commons.

Record Commission. Records of the Chancery Rolls, I John to 8 Henry VIII. Transcripts in full 1837.

Records of the Borough of Nottingham, Nottingham Local Studies Library.

Secondary Sources

Cooper, B., *Transformation of a Valley.* Heinemann, 1983. Reprinted by Scarthin Books, 1991.

Cross, F.L., Ed., *Oxford Dictionary of the Christian Church.* O.U.P. 1957.

Defoe, D. *Tour through the Whole Island of Great Britain. (1724-1726).* Everyman's Library, 1948.

Derby City Council, *Riverlife* leaflets, Derby C.C.

Farey, J., *General View of the Agriculture and Minerals of Derbyshire,* Vol. 1 (1811). Reprint by Peak District Mines Historical Society Ltd., (1989).

Fiennes, C., *The Journeys of Celia Fiennes.* Ed. by C. Morris, Cresset Press, London, 1967.

Glover, S., *History and Gazetteer of the County of Derby,* Vol. 1. 1829.

Phillips, *Phillips Inland Navigation, 1805.* Reprint by David & Charles, 1970.

Saltman, A., Ed., *Cartulary of Dale Abbey, Vol. 2.* Derbyshire Archaeological Society Record Series, 1967.

Walton, I. & Cotton, C., *The Complete Angler. 1676.* Samuel Bagster, London, 1808.

Woolley, W., *History of Derbyshire, 1712.* Ed. by Glover, C. & Riden, P., Derbyshire Record Society, Vol. VI, 1981.

Notes

Abbreviations

D.A.J.	Derbyshire Archaeological Journal.
D.L.S.L.	Derby Local Studies Library.
D.N.B.	Dictionary of National Biography.
D.R.O.	Derbyshire Record Office.
H.M.C.	Historical Manuscripts Commission.
J.H.C.	Journals of the House of Commons.
R.B.N.	Records of the Borough of Nottingham.
S.R.O.	Staffordshire Record Office.

Introduction

Numbers refer to numbers in parentheses at end of paragraphs.

1. Farey, J., *General View of the Agriculture and Minerals of Derbyshire,* Vol. I. (1811), p.4, 11-72.

   Defoe, D., *Tour through the Whole Island of Great Britain,* (1724-26), p.457-479, *passim.*

   Fiennes, C., *The Journeys of Celia Fiennes, Northern Journey (3)* 1697, p.103.

   Walton, I. & Cotton, C., *The Complete Angler,* Part II, p.378 & p.389.

Chapter 1

2. Charter of King John, granted to the Burgesses of Derby 1204. Transcript printed by the Record Commission, 1837, p.138.
   For comments about the nine mills at Borrowash, see:- Introduction to *The Cartulary of Dale Abbey,* p.17, Footnote, 79; Colvin, H. M., *Dale Abbey, Granges, Mills and other Buildings,* D.A.J. 1939. p.152.
3. *Oxford Dictionary of the Christian Church,* cv. Prebend.
4. This, and the following three paragraphs are based on the D.N.B. and family manuscripts.
5. Lothian, X94/57/1/1; H.M.C. Cowper, Vol. 2, 57/19;

Chapter 2

6. J.H.C. Vol. 9; R.B.N. Vol. 5.
7. This, and the following two paragraphs are based on R.B.N. Vol. 5.
8. Lothian, X94/57/135/4; R.B.N. Vol. 5.
9. Lothian, X94/57/- *passim.*
10. J.H.C. Vol. 12; Lothian, X94/57/1/4, 11.

Chapter 3

11. Lothian, X94/57/4/5,6,9,10.
12. Lothian, X94/57/4/13,14; 57/1/8; 57/8/1,2.
13. Lothian, X94/57/1/5.
14. Lothian, X94/57/1/10.
15. R.B.N. Vol. 6; J.H.C. Vol. 14.
16. Lothian, X94/57/4/20,21.
17. Lothian, X94/57/8/3; 57/1/6; 57/1/14; 2/-, or two shillings, on decimalization in 1973 became 10p.
18. R.B.N. Vol. 6; Catton, D3155/WH/2235.

Chapter 4

19. Catton, D3155/WH/2232, 2238, 2239, 2249.
20. Catton, D3155/WH/2257, 2261.
21. S.R.O., D593/9/16/1/14; Catton, D3155/WH/2250, 2254, 2257, 2260, 2261, 2244, 2255, 2253.
22. J.H.C. Vol. 19; Catton, D3155/WH/2274.
23. Catton, D3155/WH/2262, 2274, 2279.
24. Catton, D3155/WH/2269, 2270, 2272, 2281.
25. Catton, D3155/WH/2231.

Chapter 5

26. This, and the following three paragraphs are based on Catton, D3155/WH/2207, 2236, 2237.
27. D.L.S.L., *Derby Postman* Vol. 1, No. 8.
28. Harpur-Crewe, D2375/M/64/17; Lothian, X94/57/5/10;
29. D.L.S.L., *Derby Postman*, supra.
30. Lothian, X94/57/8/5.
31. D.R.O., D533A/TT4; Lothian, X94/57/8/7, 57/234/1/26, 30, 57/234/2/1.
32. D.R.O., D533A/TT1, 2, 5 to 15; D533A/TC/282.
33. D.L.S.L., *Derby Mercury*, Jan. 23rd. 1767.
34. Catton, D3155/WH/2223; Harpur-Crewe, D2375/87/26.

Chapter 6

35. D.R.O., D769/B/P/13/3/1; Glover. S., *History and Gazetteer of the County of Derby,* Vol. I, p.270.
36. This, and the following three paragraphs refer to the Derby Canal Act 1793, see D.R.O., D769/B/12/13/1.
37. Harpur-Crewe, D2375/87/26; Catton, D3155/WH/2223; *Phillips Inland Navigation 1805,* p.291.
38. D.R.O., D769/B/P/13/3/1/82, 430-433.
39. Derby City Council, *Riverlife* leaflets; Woolley, W., *History of Derbyshire,* 1712, p.31.

Index

(Numbers in italics refer to illustrations)

Also published by Scarthin Books

Walls Across the Valley - The Building of the Howden and Derwent Dams. Brian Robinson.
An illustrated history of the work of the Derwent Valley Water Board. Contains a wealth of previously unpublished photographs. Of particular interest to students of social, local, railway and engineering history.

Historic Farmhouses Around Derby. Barbara Hutton.
A detailed study of the old brick and timber farmhouses of South Derbyshire and the Trent Valley. Photographs, plans and line drawings, full gazetteer/index.

Millclose: The Mine that Drowned. Lynn Willies, Keith Gregory, Harry Parker.
The story of Britain's largest ever lead mine and the men who worked it. 59 illustrations. Published jointly with the Peak District Mines Historical Society to mark the 50th anniversary of the mine's closure.

Pauper's Venture: Children's Fortune. The Lead Mines and Miners of Brassington. Ron Slack.
A study of the lead-mining community of Brassington, with gazetteer of sites.

St. John's Chapel, Belper: The Life of a Church and a Community. E. G. Power.
The history of "The Foresters' Chapel" and the people it served, from the thirteenth century to the present day.

The Crich Tales: Unexpurgated Echoes from a Derbyshire Village. Geoffrey Dawes.
Tales of earthy humour and rural shrewdness, told in a village pub, with original illustrations by Geoff Taylor.

Our Village: Alison Uttley's Cromford. Alison Uttley.
Selected essays, illustrated by C. F. Tunnicliffe, vividly recalling the village scenes of her childhood.

Hanged for a Sheep: Crime in Bygone Derbyshire. E. G. Power.
A factual but entertaining survey of crime and the fight against it c. 1750-1850.

Robert Bakewell: Artist Blacksmith. S. Dunkerley.
Bound in high-quality cloth. Thirty-two pages of colour photographs with opposing pages of commentary from the core of this unique life of the great eighteenth century craftsman in wrought iron. With explanatory line drawings, gazetteer and index. Limited to 750 signed copies.

Transformation of a Valley. Brian Cooper.
A study of the growth of industry along the Derbyshire Derwent. Hardbound with full-colour dustjacket and numerous illustrations and maps.

Scarthin Books also publish

The Family Walks Series.
Each book has sixteen short, circular walks carefully chosen to appeal to children, with plenty of wildlife, historical and general interest, and stops for play, rest and refreshment.

Full Catalogue free on request from Scarthin Books, Cromford, Derbyshire DE4 3QF.

Scarthin Books of Cromford are the leading Peak District Specialists in secondhand and antiquarian books, and are particularly interested in local history, architecture and industrial archaeology.
Contact: Dr. D. J. Mitchell.

WATERWAYS TO DERBY
© *Celia M. Swainson 1993*
No part of this book may be reproduced in any form or by any means without the permission of the Owner of the Copyright.
ISBN 0 907758 48 7